THE COMMON LAW LIBRARY

D1380719

CHARLESWORTH & PERCY

ON

NEGLIGENCE

FIRST SUPPLEMENT
TO THE THIRTEENTH EDITION

Edited by

C.T. Walton, MA (Cantab)

Formerly a Circuit Judge on the North-Eastern Circuit

Richard Hyde, PhD

*Solicitor (Non-Practicing), Assistant Professor of Law,
University of Nottingham*

Up to date to 8 July 2015

SWEET & MAXWELL  THOMSON REUTERS

Published in 2015 by Thomson Reuters (Professional) UK Limited
trading as Sweet & Maxwell, Friars House, 160 Blackfriars Road,
London SE1 8EZ
(Registered in England & Wales, Company No 1679046.
Registered Office and address for service:
2nd Floor, 1 Mark Square, Leonard Street, London EC2A 4EG)

For further information on our products and services, visit:
www.sweetandmaxwell.co.uk

Typeset by Wright and Round Ltd., Gloucester
Printed and bound by CPI Group (UK) Ltd, Croydon CR0 4YY

Main Work 9780414034235
First Supplement 9780414052772

No natural forests were destroyed
to make this product; only farmed
timber was used and replanted

A CIP catalogue record for this book
is available from the British Library

HOW TO USE THIS SUPPLEMENT

The First Supplement to the Thirteenth Edition of *Charlesworth & Percy on Negligence* is ordered according to the structure of the Main Volume.

At the beginning of the supplementary coverage for each Chapter the mini Table of Contents from the Main Volume has been included. Where a heading on this Table of Contents has been marked with a black square pointer then there is relevant information in the Supplement to which you should refer. A white square pointer indicates material that has been included from the previous Supplement.

Within each Chapter updating information is referenced to the relevant paragraph in the Main Volume. The instructions in the square brackets explain how the added material relates to the Main Volume.

TABLE OF CASES

TABLE OF STATUTORY INSTRUMENTS

TABLE OF CIVIL PROCEDURE RULES

TABLE OF EUROPEAN DIRECTIVES

TABLE OF EUROPEAN AND INTERNATIONAL

CHAPTER 1

THE MEANING OF NEGLIGENCE

2.—NEGLIGENCE AS CARELESS CONDUCT

Negligence and "accident"

[*Add to line 3 of n.17*]   **1–10**

. . . suffered serious injury); also *Dunnage v Randall* [2015] EWCA Civ 673 (a similarly-worded insurance policy covered injuries suffered by the claimant when he attempted to prevent his uncle, who was suffering paranoid schizophrenia, setting fire to himself: the uncle's actions were not wilful or malicious because he had lost control of his ability to make choices and could not be said to have intended to injure the appellant, but objectively the uncle was in breach of his duty of care to the claimant and what happened was correctly characterised as an accident). [For the meaning . . .

3.—NEGLIGENCE AS THE BREACH OF A DUTY TO TAKE CARE

The third meaning

[*Add new footnote reference 42a to "objectively" in line 2*]   **1–19**

NOTE 42a. See *Dunnage v Randall* [2015] EWCA Civ 673, para. 1-10, n.17, above (the disturbed mental state of someone who attempted to set fire to himself did not prevent his owing a duty of care towards another person who attempted to rescue him).

Actionability

[*Add to the end of n.78*]   **1–30**

See also *Greenway & Ors v Johnson Matthey Plc* [2015] P.I.Q.R. P10 (where, in breach of duty, the defendant's employees were exposed to platinum salts in the course of their employment and thereby sensitised to allergy, they could not claim for loss of earnings or earnings capacity where no allergy had in fact developed before their exposure ceased and their condition was and would remain symptomless).

THE DUTY TO TAKE CARE

1.—THE CONCEPT OF A DUTY OF CARE

(B) Duty formulae

History

2–05   [*Add new footnote to text*]

"Cause of action" is a term that will recur throughout this work. Per Diplock LJ in *Letang v Cooper* [1965] 1 Q.B. 232 at 242 it is used to, "describe the various categories of factual situations which entitle[d] one person to obtain from the court a remedy against another." (quoted by Arden LJ in *Clark v In Focus Asset Management & Tax Solutions Ltd* [2014] P.N.L.R. 19, CA at [4]).

(C) Application of the Caparo analysis

Duty to the claimant

2–39   [*Note 86*]

Thompson v Renwick Group Plc reported at [2014] P.I.Q.R. P18, CA.

2.—THE KIND OF CONDUCT

(B) Omissions

Known dangers

2–71   [*Add to n.143*]

See also *Coope v Ward* [2015] EWCA Civ 30 (neighbouring landowners owed each other a measured duty of care in respect of the consequences of the collapse of a wall between their adjoining properties, even though the collapse itself did not arise as a result their fault; nevertheless it was not fair, just and reasonable to impose on one party a liability to contribute to the cost of some as yet unspecified engineering solution and in particular it was unreasonable to compel that party to contribute to the construction of a wall which was entirely on the other's land and from which they would derive no benefit other than the removal of the risk of a further collapse).

Inducing reliance

[*Note 179*]   2–80

Thompson v Renwick Group Plc reported at [2014] P.I.Q.R. P18, CA.

Voluntary assumption

[*Add to n.214*]   2–95

[2011] 1 F.L.R. 1361, CA,] Chap 12, para.12-18, below.

[*Add to n.215*]

. . . of the charge).] See also *Sebry v Companies House* [2015] EWHC 115 (QB) where it was held that the registrar of companies owed a duty of care when entering a winding-up order on the companies register, to take reasonable care to ensure that the order was not registered against the wrong company. (The claimant company was wrongly recorded on the register as having been wound up by order of the court when it was not in liquidation; its suppliers then withdrew credit and it was subsequently placed in administration).

3.—THE KIND OF HARM

(A) Introduction

[*Note 223*]   2–100

Robinson v Chief Constable of West Yorkshire reported at [2014] P.I.Q.R. P14, CA.

(B) Physical damage claims

Physical change

[*Add to the end of n.229*]   2–102

See also *Greenway & Ors v Johnson Matthey Plc* [2015] P.I.Q.R. P10, Chap 1, para.1-30, above.

Engaging with the enemy

[*Add to n.258*]   2–114

. . . 130 L.Q.R. 28]; also Fairgrieve, "Suing the military: the justiciability of damages claims against the armed forces" C.L.J. 2014, 73(1), 18.

Police operations

2–117   [*Note 264*]

Robinson v Chief Constable of West Yorkshire reported at [2014] P.I.Q.R. P14,
CA.

(C) Psychiatric injury

Intentionally inflicted mental injury

2–130a   [*Add new paragraph to text*]

In *Rhodes v MLA*,[298a] the Supreme Court considered whether the publication
of a semi-autobiographical book by a celebrity graphically disclosing past
incidents of abuse, where such disclosures would cause harm to the defendant's autistic infant son, would fall within the rule in *Wilkinson v Downton*.
It was held that the tort of wilful infringement of the right to personal safety
(as the tort in *Wilkinson v Downton* should be known) has three elements; a
conduct element; a mental element; and a consequence element.[298b] The
conduct element "requires words or conduct directed towards the claimant for
which there is no justification or reasonable excuse."[298c] In general "it is
difficult to envisage any circumstances in which speech which is not
deceptive, threatening or possibly abusive, could give rise to liability in tort,"
and the true words published in the instant case could not constitute the
conduct element of the tort.[298d] The mental element requires the claimant to
demonstrate that the defendant had an actual "intention to cause physical
harm or severe mental or emotional distress."[298e] Recklessness will not
suffice, and imputed intention has "no proper role in the modern law of
tort."[298f] The consequence element requires that the claimant demonstrate that
they have suffered physical harm or recognised psychiatric illness as a result
of the conduct. The continuing utility of the tort, in doubt following the
judgment of Lord Hoffmann in Wainwright which suggested that Wilkinson
had "no leading role in the modern law," was confirmed,[298g] as "negligence
and intent are very different fault elements and there are principled reasons for
differentiating between the bases (and possible extent) of liability for causing
personal injury in either case."[298h]
Note 298a. [2015] 2 W.L.R. 1373 SC.
Note 298b. Ibid. para [88].
Note 298c. Ibid. para [74].
Note 298d. Ibid. para [77].
Note 298e. Ibid. para [87].
Note 298f. Ibid. para [81].
Note 298g. *Wainwright v Home Office* [2004] 2 AC 406, 425, para [41].
Note 298h. *Rhodes v MLA* para [63].

Proximity in time and space

2–153   [*Add to the end of n.339*]

; *Baker v Cambridgeshire and Peterborough NHS Foundation Trust* [2015]
EWHC 609 (QB) at [41].

Later consequences of accident

[*Add new paragraph to text*]   **2–154a**

Taylor v A Novo was applied in *Wild v Southend University Hospital NHS Foundation Trust*.[341a] A father suffered psychiatric injury due to his presence during the stillbirth of his child, although he had not been present at the time of the negligence that led to the death of the foetus in the womb. His claim for damages for psychiatric injury therefore failed, as he was not present to witness the shocking event in question, but had only a witnessed the consequence of the injury sustained at that time. The mother was able to recover for her psychiatric injury and it might be thought unsatisfactory to have in effect a gender divide in pre-natal negligence cases, with mothers being able to recover damages, and fathers frequently not, albeit suffering a similar injury. Further, taken with *Taylor*, the case illustrates that it is easier to recover for psychiatric injury sustained as a result of witnessing injuries caused by an accident, rather than witnessing injuries resulting from industrial diseases or clinical negligence, where those injuries may not become apparent until years after the event.

NOTE 341a. [2014] EWHC 4053 (QB), Michael Kent QC (sitting as a Judge of the High Court). See Allen, "Nervous shock: a "most vexed and tantalising topic" . . . still" 2015 J.P.I.L. (1), 1.

Shock-induced injury

[*Add to n.345*]   **2–156**

See further *Liverpool Women's Hospital NHS Foundation Trust v Ronayne* [2015] EWCA Civ 588, n.350, below (no "horrifying event" where the appearance of the claimant's wife when he saw her in hospital before and after surgery was not exceptional by objective standards).

Suddenness

[*Add to n.349*]   **2–157**

There was no sudden and direct appreciation of a horrifying event where the claimant, over a period of time, was informed in telephone messages or in a face-to face conversation with her sister's husband, of her sister's deteriorating, and ultimately fatal, medical condition: *Shorter v Surrey and Sussex Healthcare NHS Trust* [2015] EWHC 614 (QB) (*per* Swift J., it was necessary to be cautious in finding that when the claimant saw her sister on a hospital trolley towards the start of the period she was in hospital, the claimant's professional expertise as a nurse made the sight more horrifying than it would have been to a person without her knowledge: the "event" had to be one that would be recognised as horrifying by a person of ordinary susceptibility; in other words, by objective standards).

[*Add to n.350*]   **2–158**

Contrast *Liverpool Women's Hospital NHS Foundation Trust v Ronayne* [2015] EWCA Civ 588 (no "seamless tale" where over the period of time the claimant's wife was in hospital there was a series of events as her condition deteriorated and in advance of two particularly distressing visits he was given information in advance of what to expect).

Work-related stress

2–167   [*Add to n.366 after the reference to Dickins v O2 Plc*]

... [2009] I.R.L.R. 58, CA]; *Daniel v Secretary of State for the Department of Health* [2014] EWHC 2578 (QB); *Yapp v Foreign and Commonwealth Office* [2015] I.R.L.R. 112, CA. [See generally ...

(E) Negligent statements causing financial injury

Reasonable reliance

2–194   [*Add to text after n.431*]

There can be no true reliance where the statement which forms the basis of the claim does not come into existence until after the claimant has taken the action said to have been taken in reliance on it.[431a] So, claims against property consultants based on defects in properties for which certificates of proper construction had been provided, failed, the leaseholders having purchased their interest in the properties before the certificates were seen by them: that being so they could not have relied on any negligent misstatement the certificates contained at the time they committed themselves to purchase.[431b] It has also been held that it would not be reasonable for a commercial lender such as a bank to rely on statements from a solicitor regarding the affairs of their mutual client, without checking the accuracy of such information, and a competent solicitor would not have foreseen that the bank would rely on such statements.[431c]

NOTE 431a. *Hunt v Optima (Cambridge) Ltd* [2014] P.N.L.R. 29, CA.
NOTE 431b. *ibid.*
NOTE 431c. *NRAM plc v Steel* [2014] CSOH 172.

Proximity of relationship

2–195   [*Add to the end of n.433*]

See further *Swynson Ltd v Lowick Rose LLP* [2014] P.N.L.R. 27, para. 2-204a, below (no duty owed to a director of a company in respect of advice given to that company).

Company auditors

2–199   [*Add new footnote 445a to "company" in the last line*]

NOTE 445a. An auditor engaged to carry out non-statutory audits may owe a duty to third parties other than the members of a company in general meeting, see *Barclays Bank plc v Grant Thornton UK LLP* [2015] EWHC 320 *per* Cooke J at [50]-[54], although on the facts no duty was owed in light of a disclaimer inserted into the audit reports produced by the defendant.

Company directors

2–204a   [*Add new paragraph to text*]

A situation which can be seen as the converse of *Williams v Natural Life Health Foods Ltd*[454a] arose in *Swynson Ltd v Lowick Rose LLP*,[454b] where the defendant accountants firm were held not to owe a personal duty to a company director in respect of advice given to the company, notwithstanding that it was foreseeable that the director may suffer loss as a result of negligent advice given by them. It makes no difference if the company has a single owner who is also the director of the company.

NOTE 454a. [1998] 1 W.L.R. 830, HL.

NOTE 454b. [2014] P.N.L.R. 27.

[*Add new footnote reference 456a to "obscure" in the last line*] **2–206**

NOTE 456a. The approach in *Williams v Natural Life Health Foods Ltd* was applied in preference to *Merrett v Babb* in *Summit Advances Ltd v Bush* [2015] P.N.L.R. 18 (mortgage lenders were unsuccessful in their contention that a surveyor employed by a limited liability partnership owed them a personal duty of care in relation to a valuation of property prepared by him in the course of that employment).

Disclaimers

[*Add to text after n.482*] **2–213**

In *Barclays Bank plc v Grant Thornton UK LLP*[482a] a disclaimer appearing on the first page of a non-statutory audit report, which followed a standard form produced by the Institute of Chartered Accountants in England & Wales in respect of statutory audits, save for changing "the company's members" to "the company's director[s]", was held sufficient to prevent a duty of care arising to the third party bank.

NOTE 482a. [2015] EWHC 320 (Comm).

Unfair Contract Terms Act 1977

[*Add new footnote reference 482a after "1977" in the heading*] **2–214**

NOTE 482a. Where one party is a consumer and the other is a trader the Unfair Contract Terms Act 1977 will cease to have effect upon the coming into force of the Consumer Rights Act 2015. The Unfair Terms in Consumer Contracts Regulation 1999 will also be repealed, and the provisions consolidated with the consumer provisions of the Unfair Contract Terms Act in Part 2 of the Consumer Rights Act. Terms which seek to exclude or restrict liability in respect of personal injury or death are void (s.65). Other terms which seek to exclude liability in negligence, for example for property damage or economic loss, will be subjected to a test of fairness (s.62). The Act provides guidance on the meaning of unfairness (ss. 62, 63 and schedule 2). The Unfair Contract Terms Act will continue to apply to contracts made between two businesses in a modified form. The amendments to the 1977 Act are set out in Schedule 4 of the Consumer Rights Act.

[*Add new footnote reference 486a to "factors" in line 12*]

NOTE 486a. See also *Barclays Bank plc v Grant Thornton UK LLP* [2015] EWHC 320, *per* Cooke J at [55] to [91].

(F) Negligent conduct causing financial injury

Third party payments

2–219 [*Add new footnote 490a to"reasonable" in the last line*]

NOTE 490a. See further, *Network Rail Infrastructure Ltd v Handy* [2015] EWHC 1175 (TCC).

Balancing policy concerns

2–233 [*Add to n.518*]

See also *Sebry v Companies House* [2015] EWHC 115 (QB), Edis J., n.215, above (in imposing a duty of care upon the register of companies in relation to the accuracy of an entry on the companies register a number of factors came into account, notably that: (a) unless a remedy was provided by the common law of negligence, a company damaged by carelessness in the particular circumstances would have no remedy; (b) it was not difficult for the registrar's staff to avoid errors of the type made; (c) there were no public policy reasons for denying a duty of care; (d) the statutory duty or contractual relationship between the company and the registrar did not limit the nature and extent of the responsibility; (e) balancing the harm done to the company against the potential adverse impact on the registrar, it was clear that the balance favoured the loss falling on the registrar rather than the company; (f) it was likely that the imposition of a duty would improve the accuracy of the register, which was plainly in the public interest.

Miscellaneous cases

2–247 [*Add new footnote reference to "relevant" in line 1*]

NOTE 555a. See further paras 2-298 and 2-329 below and Chap. 12, paras 12-05ff.

[*Note 558*]

Harrison v Technical Sign Co Ltd reported at [2014] P.N.L.R. 15.

[*Add to n.558*]

. . . shop front).] See also *Stagecoach South Western Trains v Hind* [2014] E.G.L.R. 59, Ch. 9, para. 9-311, below.

4.—THE KIND OF CLAIMANT

(C) Unborn children

Congenital Disabilities (Civil Liability) Act 1976

2–281 [*Add new footnote reference 643a to "mother" in line 5*]

NOTE 643a. See *per* Lord Dyson MR in *CP v Criminal Injuries Compensation Authority* [2015] 2 W.L.R. 463, CA, Ch. 17, para. 17-33 below, at [66]: " . . . in English law women do not owe a duty of care in tort to their unborn child.

A competent woman cannot be forced to have a caesarean section or other medical treatment to prevent potential risk to the foetus during childbirth. The negligent acts of a third party tortfeasor, which inflict harm on an unborn child, are actionable by the child on birth if the child is born with disabilities under section 1(1) of the Congenital Disabilities (Civil Liability) Act 1976 . But claims cannot be brought under this Act against the child's mother unless (by section 2) the harm is caused by her when she is driving a motor vehicle." He went on to say, in the context of a claim for criminal injuries compensation, "The law would be incoherent if a child were unable to claim compensation from her mother for breach of a duty of care owed during pregnancy, but the mother was criminally liable for causing the harm which gave rise to damage and a right to compensation under the 1995 Act."

[Add to n. 644]

For the position where a child *in utero,* injured by its mother, seeks compensation under the Criminal Injuries Compensation Scheme, see Chap. 17, para. 17-33, below.

5.—The Kind of Defendant

(E) Public bodies

The police

[Add to n.704]   **2–311**

In *B v Chief Constable of X* [2015] I.R.L.R. 284, Males J., it was observed that a Chief Constable owed a duty of care to an officer operating undercover to take reasonable steps to ensure that he did not suffer psychiatric injury as a result of the stress of his work; but there was no breach of duty on the facts, and the injury alleged by the claimant arose from his own misconduct.

[Note 707]

Robinson v Chief Constable of West Yorkshire reported at [2014] P.I.Q.R. P14, CA.

Hill and Smith

[Delete text in n.710 after the first line and replace as follows]   **2–312**

. . . *South Wales Police*] [2015] 2 W.L.R. 343, S.C., para. 2-312a, below.

[Add new paragraph to text]   **2–312a**

In *Michael v Chief Constable of South Wales*[710a] the Supreme Court confirmed the continuing applicability of the decision in *Smith*. The appellants were the parents and children of the deceased, who had been murdered by her ex-partner despite making an emergency call to the police, to which it was alleged they had failed to respond to appropriately. In the lead judgment Lord Toulson JSC held that the police did not owe a duty of care, even in circumstances where they were aware of a serious threat to an individual (which they know from the content of the deceased's emergency call) or from a particular individual (which they should also have known from the call). Imposing such duties would not be fair, just and reasonable, would lead to increased resource pressures on police forces without necessarily leading to corresponding improvements in performance, and limits on the scope of the duties would be difficult fairly to identify. Further, such duties were not compelled by article 2 of the European Convention on Human Rights, which does not require that individuals be compensated through claims in negligence in circumstances which may well also give rise to compensation for breach of the Convention. Further there was no duty owed by virtue of an assumption of responsibility. However, the claim for damages under s.7 of the Human Rights Act 1998 could proceed.[710b]

NOTE 710a. [2015] 2 W.L.R. 343, S.C.

NOTE 710b. See generally para. 2-346, below.

Fire services

2–323   [*Add to n.742*]

See further, *Mackay v Scottish Fire & Rescue Service* [2015] CSOH 55 (no duty owed to a pedestrian injured by ice falling from a tenement roof after the defender had inspected the property to establish the risk of injury posed by ice and snow which had built up on its façade: the firefighters had neither caused the situation nor made it worse and there was no assumption of responsibility to a pedestrian passing below).

Other cases

2–324a   [*Add new paragraph to text*]

A sewerage operator did not assume responsibility towards a customer in circumstances where it had engaged in the clean-up of escaped sewage from her home, because its actions did not go beyond that which was required by the statutory scheme under the Water Industry Act 1991.[748a]

NOTE 748a. *Nicholson v Thames Water Utilities Ltd* [2014] EWHC 4249 (QB), Chap. 13, para. 13-90, below.

Negligence and misfeasance

2–326   [*Add to n.755*]

... 2861, CA.] *Rowley* was applied in *Lillian Darby (Administratrix) v Richmond upon Thames LBC* [2015] EWHC 909 (QB) (a local housing authority performing its statutory duty to allocate social housing by assessing need under a points system, owed no duty of care in applying that system to the deceased, who had made a request with the support of his GP, to be re-housed since he suffered from leukaemia and was at risk of infection if he continued to live in his existing accommodation with his sister and her baby: his need was not assessed as urgent and he contracted influenza and died three weeks later).

PARTIES AND VICARIOUS LIABILITY

1.—PARTIES

(A) The Crown

Liability for negligence

[*Add to text after n.34*]   **3–11**

Since s.2 of the Crown Proceedings Act 1947 was designed to put the Crown in the same position as an ordinary private person of full age and capacity, the Home Office can be liable, by way of a non-delegable duty of care,[34a] for the negligent actions of an independent contractor.[34b]

NOTE 34a. In relation to such duties see para. 3-195, below and *Woodland v Essex County Council* [2013] 3 W.L.R. 1227, S.C.

NOTE 34b. *GB v Home Office* [2015] EWHC 819 (QB), Coulson J, para. 3-196, below.

(B) Judges and quasi judges, prosecutors, the police

Judicial acts

[*Add to n.42*]   **3–15**

An ombudsman appointed under the Financial Services and Markets Act 2000 to determine disputes between consumers and providers of financial services makes a judicial decision when making an award, see *Clark v In Focus Asset Management & Tax Solutions Ltd* [2014] P.N.L.R. 19, CA, per Arden LJ at [82].

(C) The armed forces

Other cases

[*Add to n.75*]   **3–25**

... should have been aware.] Contrast *Vaughan v Ministry of Defence* [2015] EWHC 1404 (QB) William Davis J. (the defendant did not owe a duty of care as employer, to a marine who suffered serious injuries after executing a shallow dive in the sea while off duty during a training week).

(H) Partners

Generally

3–54 *[Add to n.139]*

Further, see *Northampton Regional Livestock Centre Co Ltd v Cowling* [2015] EWCA Civ 651, para. 3-150, n.387, below.

(J) Children

Duty of care of parents

3–58 *[Add to n.153]*

See also *OPO vMLA* [2015] E.M.L.R. 4, CA, Chap. 2, para. 2-130a, above (no duty of care was owed by a father to his young son, who suffered a number of significant disabilities, not to publish an account of sexual abuse the father had suffered as a child, notwithstanding that such publication would be likely to cause his son enduring psychological harm).

(K) Prisoners and bankrupts

Prisoners

3–68 *[Note 176]*

Cox v Ministry of Justice reported at [2014] P.I.Q.R. P17, CA.

(L) Persons suffering mental disorder

Generally

3–75a *[Add new paragraph to text]*

The extent to which, if at all, profound mental disorder could prevent an individual being in breach of a duty of care was explored in *Dunnage v Randall*.[192a] The claimant suffered serious injuries in attempting unsuccessfully to prevent his uncle, who suffered disabling mental illness, from setting fire to himself. He sought to recover damages on the basis that his uncle was in breach of a duty of care towards him as a potential rescuer. On appeal it was held that, the test being objective, liability attached. A defendant impaired by medical problems, whether physical or mental, could not escape liability if he caused injury by failing to exercise reasonable care. Only a defendant whose medical incapacity had the effect of entirely eliminating any fault or responsibility for an injury to another could be excused, but that was not the position where, as here, the defendant's mind, although deluded, directed his actions.
Note 192a. [2015] EWCA Civ 673, Ch. 1, para. 1-10, above.

2.—VICARIOUS LIABILITY

(A) Employees and relationships akin to employment.

Illustrations: unskilled occupations

[*Note 282*]   **3–113**

Cox v Ministry of Justice reported at [2014] P.I.Q.R. P17, CA.

Relationships akin to employment

[*Add new paragraph to text*]   **3–118a**

In the absence of day to day control a local authority's relationship with a foster parent was not a relationship akin to employment and it was accordingly not vicariously liable for physical, emotional and sexual abuse inflicted upon a child in care by the foster parents with whom she was placed.[304a] It was said that it is an essential feature of fostering that a local authority do not have control over the actions of foster parents, as their role "is to provide family life, bringing up the child as a member of their own family" which is only possible "if a foster parent enjoys independence from direction by the local authority and autonomy to determine how the child should be parented."[304b] In effect a local authority is likely to be vicariously liable to a child injured as a result of negligence within a local authority care home, but not if the child is injured whilst placed in foster care.

NOTE 304a *NA v Nottinghamshire County Council* [2015] Fam. Law 133.
NOTE 304b ibid. per Males J at [176].

Dishonesty, fraud or other criminal act

[*Add to the end of n.387*]   **3–150**

The test in the *Dubai Aluminium* case was considered in *Northampton Regional Livestock Centre Co Ltd v Cowling* [2015] EWCA Civ 651, a claim against partners, where the issue was the liability of both partners for a breach of duty by one of them. It was observed that in such circumstances authority was not the touchstone for joint and several partnership liability. The touchstone was the connection between the wrongful conduct and the acts a partner was authorised to do, and in particular whether the connection was such that the wrongful conduct might fairly and properly be regarded as done by the partner while acting in the ordinary course of the partnership business.

[*Add to n.397*]   **3–153**

Following *Maga*, trustees of a society of Jehovah's Witnesses were vicariously liable for sexual assaults carried out by a ministerial servant on a child in the congregation, and for the failure of the elders to take reasonable steps to protect her from the abuser once they knew of his earlier abuse of another child: *A v Trustees of the Watchtower Bible and Tract Society* [2015] EWHC 1722 (QB), Globe J.

[Add to text after n.401]

... racist views;[401] nor was an employer vicariously liable where a bodyshop employee sprayed a co-worker's overalls with thinning agent, an inflammable substance, and then used a cigarette lighter in his vicinity, causing serious injury.[401a] [There was an insufficiently ...

NOTE 401a. *Graham v Commercial Bodyworks Ltd* [2015] EWCA Civ 47, considering *Vaickuviene v J Sainsbury Plc* n.401, above. While there was a risk in requiring the use of thinning agent in the course of the men's work, it could not be said that the creation of that risk was sufficiently closely connected with the highly reckless act of the guilty party.

Further examples of acts in the course of employment

3–156   *[Add to text after n.424]*

A bank was vicariously liable for the negligence of an employee who provided a positive reference to a third party stating that a customer had an account and was trustworthy to the extent of £1.6 million in any one week, when in fact, the customer's balance had always been nil.[424a]

NOTE 424a. *Playboy Club London Ltd v Banca Nazionale Del Lavoro SPA* [2014] EWHC 2613 (QB) the reference came from a business manager of the bank who had no responsibility for the account but the provision of a reference was deemed so closely connected with acts that she was authorised to do that the wrongful conduct might fairly and properly be regarded as done by her in the course of her employment).

3.—NON DELEGABLE DUTIES

(D) Special relationships

3–195   *[Note 543]*

Woodland v Essex CC reported at [2014] A.C. 537.

[Add to n.543]

See George, "Non-delegable duties of care in tort" L.Q.R. 2014, 130(Oct), 534; Morgan, "Liability for independent contractors in contract and tort: duties to ensure that care is taken" 2015 C.L.J. 74(1) 109.

3–196   *[Add new footnote reference 543a to "homes" in line 5]*

NOTE 543a. A detainee in an immigration removal centre run by an independent organisation on behalf of the Home Office, was owed a non-delegable duty of care in respect of allegedly negligent medical treatment received by her, since such detainees were inherently vulnerable and highly dependent on the observance of proper standards of care: *GB v Home Office* [2015] EWHC 819 (QB), Coulson J (a decision on a preliminary issue).

[Add to n. 544]

In addition to the factors listed it must also be fair, just and reasonable to impose a non delegable duty: for a case where it was not, even though the factors were present, see *NA v Nottinghamshire CC* [2014] EWHC 4005 (QB), para. 3-118a, above (no such duty imposed upon a local authority in relation to acts of abuse perpetrated upon a child by foster parents with whom the child had been placed, where it would have a significant resource impact and may cause local authorities to become more unwilling to place looked after children in foster care).

[Add new footnote reference 544a to "contractor" in the second last line]

NOTE 544a. The point of principle having been decided the case was remitted for trial and the claimant succeeded in establishing that her serious personal injuries were caused or materially contributed to by a breach of duty both of a lifeguard employed at the pool and a teacher, in failing to notice in time that she was in difficulties in the water: *Woodland v Maxwell* [2015] EWHC 273 (QB).

CHAPTER 4

PRINCIPAL DEFENCES AND DISCHARGES FROM LIABILITY

1.—CONTRIBUTORY NEGLIGENCE

Share in responsibility for the damage

4–25   *[Add to the end of note 66]*

... and *Jackson v Murray* [2015] 2 All E.R. 805, SC, para. 4–40, below, per Lord Reed at [20]-[21].

Seat belts

4–27   *[Add to n.71]*

The Motor Vehicles (Wearing of Seat Belts) Regulations 1993 have been amended with effect from 1 April 2015 by the Motor Vehicles (Wearing of Seat Belts) (Amendment) (No. 2) Regulations 2015 (SI 2015/574).

Children: degree of care to be expected

4–40   *[Add to n.119]*

Compare *Jackson v Murray* [2015] 2 All E.R. 805, SC (the contributory negligence of a child of 13 was assessed at 50% where she stepped out from behind a school bus into the path of an oncoming car where poor light conditions made it difficult to assess the speed of the car which was too fast in the circumstances).

Intoxication

4–48   *[Add to note 144 after "railway" in the first line]*

... railway);] *McCaughey v Mullan* [2014] NIQB 132. [See also ...

Motor accidents

4–54   *[Add to n.159]*

... and see *Jackson v Murray* [2015] 2 All E.R. 805, SC, *per* Lord Reed at [39]-[43].

[Add to text after n.159]   **4–55**

There was no finding of contributory negligence where a motorcyclist had been travelling within the speed limit, even though it could be shown that if he had been travelling slower the accident could have been avoided.[165a]
NOTE 165a *Russell v National Farmers' Union Mutual Insurance Society Ltd* [2014] CSOH 157.

2.—AGREEMENT TO RUN THE RISK: "VOLENTI NON FIT INJURIA"

Contracting out of or limiting liability

[Add to n.277]   **4–85**

For changes to the Unfair Contract Terms Act 1977 on the coming into force of the Consumer Rights Act 2015 see para. 2-214, n.482a, above.

4.—LIMITATION OF ACTION

(A) General Principles

Economic loss

[Add new paragraph to text]   **4–158a**

A distinction drawn, when considering the accrual of a cause of action in claims of professional negligence, between "no transaction" cases and "wrong transaction" cases, was considered by the Privy Council in *Maharaj v Johnson*.[505a] In giving the leading judgment Lord Wilson said that such a distinction was a helpful signpost towards the correct outcome rather than a determinative principle in its own right. It was essential to bear in mind that the central concept behind the two types of case was different. In the "wrong"- he preferred "flawed" - transaction case the claimant entered a flawed transaction in circumstances in which, in the absence of the defendant's breach of duty, he would have entered into an analogous, but flawless, transaction. In the "no transaction" case the claimant also entered into a transaction but in circumstances in which, in the absence of the defendant's breach of duty, he would have entered into "no transaction" at all. He went on[505b]:

> "The difference in concept dictates a difference in the inquiry as to whether, and if so when, the claimant suffered actual or measurable damage. In the "flawed transaction" case the inquiry is whether the value to the claimant of the flawed transaction was measurably less than what would have been the value to him of the flawless transaction. In the "no transaction" case the inquiry is whether, and if so at what point, the transaction into which the claimant entered caused his financial position to be measurably worse than if he had not entered into it . . . "

Nykredit Mortgage Bank plc v Edward Erdman Group Ltd[505c] was an example of a "no transaction" case in that the claimants, who lent money on security of a property which valuers negligently overvalued for them, would otherwise have declined to make the loan.

NOTE 505a. [2015] UKPC 28 (an allegation that solicitors were negligent in failing to advise the claimants that a purported conveyance of land was ineffective to pass title to them since it was executed on behalf of someone who only held the land in the capacity of personal representative: when the claimants themselves attempted to sell the land many years later their questionable title was discovered and the transaction did not proceed).

NOTE 505b. Ibid at [19]. Observations in *Pegasus Management Holdings SCA v Ernst and Young* [2010] PNLR 438, CA and *Baker v Ollard and Bentley* 126 SJ 593, to the effect that if a transaction was flawed that of itself meant that the claimant suffered actual damage on entry into it, were criticised as going too far.

NOTE 505c. [1997] 1 WLR 1627, HL.

(B) Personal Injury litigation

Knowledge

4–188   *[Add to text after n.609]*

... inappropriate forceps.[609]] Where it was alleged that elders of a society of Jehovah's Witnesses had negligently failed to protect the claimant from sexual abuse at the hands of a minister to the society when she was a child, it was accepted she did not have actual knowledge of that failure until the exchange of witness statements in her assault claim.[609a]

NOTE 609a. *A v Trustees of the Watchtower Bible and Tract Society* [2015] EWHC 1722 (QB), Globe J, Ch. 3, para 3-153, above.

Constructive knowledge

4–191   *[Add to n.615]*

It was reasonable to expect a person suffering from hearing loss to ask his specialist whether a history of noise exposure which they discussed had caused or contributed to his symptoms: *Platt v BRB (Residuary) Ltd* [2015] P.I.Q.R. P7, CA (had he done so, he would probably have been informed that his tinnitus and hearing loss were noise related and he thereby had constructive knowledge of the cause of his injury more than three years before a claim was commenced.

Importance of prejudice

4–208   *[Delete "646a" in line 5]*

All the circumstances of the case

4–215a   *[Add new paragraphs to text]*

Section 33(3) directs the court to consider "all the circumstances of the case" in addition to the factors specifically set out. The interplay between the two was considered in *Collins v Secretary of State for Business Innovation and Skills*,[706a] where it was observed that one relevant circumstance was pre limitation delay, that is delay before a cause of action accrued to the claimant, and the existing authorities did not discuss its relevance at any great length. While the primary factors to consider were those set out in s.33(3)(a) to (f), pre-limitation period effluxion of time was also a relevant factor, although of less weight. Both parties could rely upon it for different purposes. A claimant might argue that it buttressed a case under s.33(3)(b); it may be said that recent delay had had little or no impact on the cogency of the evidence, the damage being done before any delay arose. The defendant could rely on the passage of time to show that it already faced massive difficulties in defending the action, and that any additional problems caused by the claimant's recent delay were therefore a serious matter. It was for the court to assess those and similar considerations before deciding on which side of the scales that factor should be placed.[706b]

In a noise induced deafness claim where it was accepted that the claimant had **4–215b** constructive knowledge sufficient to start the limitation clock ticking in 2001, but he continued in the same work thereafter for a period of three years and did not issue proceedings for a further ten, it was held that the exercise of discretion under s.33 should address two periods of time, before and after 2001. The three year period for injury sustained by 2001 expired in 2004 and there was prejudicial delay for five years after that before the claim was notified; likewise there was delay, albeit to a lesser extent, in relation to the injury sustained after 2001. All the circumstances had to be considered and care taken to give appropriate weight to pre limitation delay, also to delay after the claimant acquired knowledge, rather than focusing solely on the delay from the end of the limitation period. The Court of Appeal re-exercised the discretion and held it would be inequitable to allow the claim to proceed.[706c]

NOTE 706a. [2014] P.I.Q.R. P19, CA.

NOTE 706b. Per Jackson LJ at [66]. On the facts the trial judge had rightly declined to exercise discretion under s.33 where the claimant was guilty of some six years delay after acquiring constructive knowledge connecting his inoperable lung cancer to his exposure to asbestos between thirty and forty years earlier.

NOTE 706c. *Malone v Relyon Heating Engineering Ltd* [2014] EWCA Civ 904.

Walkley v Precision Forgings Ltd

[n.719] **4–220**

Davidson v Aegis Defence Services (BVI) Ltd reported at [2014] 2 All E.R. 216, CA.

Limitation period not disapplied.

[Add to text at the end of the paragraph] **4–222**

The limitation period was not disapplied where the claimant alleged noise induced hearing loss against his former employer, a company which had been placed into liquidation over one year before he gave notice of his potential claim, where relevant personnel and occupational health records had been

destroyed (in breach of normal document retention procedures) prior to the issue of proceeding, and no evidence could be procured from the company's former directors.[727a]
NOTE 727a. *Malone v Relyon Heating Engineering Ltd* [2014] EWCA Civ 904, para. 4–215b, above.

Defendant company no longer in existence.

4–225   *[Add to n.741]*

The discretion under s.1032(3) was considered in *Davy v Pickering* [2015] EWHC 380 (Ch).

(C) Latent Damage

Knowledge

4–232   *[Add to n.779]*

... investigated as well.] See further *Schumann v Veale Wasbrough* [2015] EWCA Civ 441 (for purposes of an allegation of professional negligence against solicitors and a barrister who advised her not to proceed with a wrongful birth claim the claimant would have had constructive knowledge that the advice was wrong long before she consulted other lawyers; in any event the original advice had been correct).

[Add to text after n.780]

... had not read it.[780]] Also, for purposes of a claim against a financial advisor who allegedly gave negligent advice to the claimant to invest in an investment bond, time ran from the date when she might reasonably have been expected to learn that she had suffered damage in that return of the amount invested was not guaranteed.[780a] Mere uncertainty about the quantification of a loss does not mean that the claimant can take advantage of section 14A.[780b]
[It is not reasonable ...
NOTE 780a. *Jacobs v Sesame Ltd.* [2015] P.N.L.R. 6, CA (Tomlinson LJ referred at [27] to the important guidance given in relation to s.14A (10) by Arden LJ in *Gravgaard v Aldridge & Brownlee*, n.779, above).
NOTE 780b. *Toombs v Bridging Loans Ltd* [2014] EWHC 4566 (QB).

(D) Miscellaneous Limitation Periods

Periods of limitation prescribed by other Acts

4–237   *[Add to n.792]*

Neither a consent order after a claimant accepted a defendant's Pt 36 offer, or a later costs order, constituted a "judgment" in a personal injury claim by which the defendant was held liable to the claimant for his injuries, and therefore did not fall within s.10(3) of the 1980 Act: *Chief Constable of Hampshire v Southampton City Council* [2015] P.I.Q.R. P5, CA.

[Add to n.296]   **4–238**

See *Feest v South West SHA* [2014] 1 Lloyd's Rep. 419 where, in considering the limitation period of two years under arts 14 and 16 of the Athens Convention of 1974, the court drew attention to the words of Lord Macmillan in *Stag Line v Foscolo Mango & Co Ltd* [1932] A.C. 328 that in construing the Hague rules "their interpretation should not be rigidly controlled by precedents of antecedent date, but rather . . . should be construed on broad principles of general acceptation."

5.—OTHER DEFENCES

(A) Henderson v Henderson

Nature of the test

[Add to n.838]   **4–250**

See also *Ridgewood Properties Group Ltd v Kilpatrick Stockton LLP* [2014] P.N.L.R. 31 (the administration of justice would be brought into disrepute if the claimants were permitted to re-litigate against a different party, issues decided against them in an earlier judgment which they had not appealed).

Irrelevant factors

[Add to n.842]   **4–253**

. . . against a tortfeasor)]; also *Ridgewood Properties Group Ltd v Kilpatrick Stockton LLP* [2014] P.N.L.R. 31 (it would bring the administration of justice into disrepute to permit the claimant to seek as damages against its former legal advisors, loss which it had failed to recover in an earlier action against different parties where it wished essentially to challenge the factual findings in the earlier proceedings.

Merger and res judicata

[Note 845]   **4–254**

Clark v In Focus Asset Management & Tax Solutions Ltd reported at [2014] P.N.L.R. 19, CA.

(B) Illegality

Generally

[Add new footnote reference 853a to "principles" in the last line]   **4–258**

NOTE 853a. The nature of the act required to engage the *ex turpi causa* defence was considered in *Les Laboratoires Servier v Apotex Inc* [2015] A.C. 430. See particularly Lord Sumption JSC at [23] onwards: whether an act was of a quality to engage the defence depended upon its legal character; criminal acts were sufficient, but also quasi criminal acts, that is, other wrongful acts which engaged the public interest. Quasi criminal acts included "cases of dishonesty or corruption, which have always been regarded as engaging the public interest even in the context of purely civil disputes; some anomalous categories of misconduct, such as prostitution, which without itself being criminal are contrary to public policy and involve criminal liability on the part of secondary parties; and the infringement of statutory rules enacted for the protection of the public interest and attracting civil sanctions of a penal character, such as the competition law . . . "

Gray v Thames Trains Ltd

4–259   [*Add to n.855*]

. . . 159 N.L.J. 1200]; Goudkamp and Zou, "The defence of illegality in tort law: beyond judicial redemption?" 2015 C.L.J. 74(1) 13. [*Gray* was applied . . .

The wider rule

4–261   [*Add to n.864*]

The *ex turpi causa* rule defeated claims by two passengers who jumped from a moving taxi in order to avoid paying the fare: *Beaumont v Ferrer* [2015] P.I.Q.R. P2, Chap. 6, para. 6-92, below. In applying the rule Kenneth Parker J was not persuaded that proportionality (as between the claimant's misconduct and the result if he were denied a remedy) had a part to play: "[38] . . . There is considerable doubt whether the Court should seek to weigh the degree and culpability of the claimant's criminality against the conduct of the defendant, and to allow a remedy if the Court concluded that the defendant's conduct was by far the more culpable. *Clerk and Lindsell on Torts* (20th edn. 2010) at 3–37 sets out powerful objections to the incorporation of "proportionality" in the relevant sense in the public policy underpinned by *ex turpi causa*, and it appears to me that the recent case of *Joyce v O'Brien* [2012] EWHC 1324 (QB); [20131 EWCA Civ 546 tends to support the proposition that 'proportionality' has ordinarily no role to play." See further, Tavares, "Beaumont v Ferrer: personal injury - road traffic accidents" J.P.I. Law 2014, 4, C211.

[*Add to the end of n.867*]

See also *McCracken v Smith* [2015] EWCA Civ 380. Where two 16-year-old boys rode a trials motorbike designed only for one rider, neither wore a crash hat and it was driven too fast down a cycle path into collision with a minibus, the ex turpi principle was applied so as to prevent the boy who was a passenger suing the driver of the bike for his injuries. He could, however recover against the driver of the minibus who had himself been negligent in failing to keep a proper look-out. The conduct which gave rise to the ex turpi defence was one of two causes of the collision, the minibus driver's negligence being the other. The correct approach was to give effect to both causes by allowing the passenger to claim in negligence against the driver of the minibus but to reduce any damages for contributory negligence. The correct deduction was 65% of which 15% reflected the failure to wear a helmet.

Stone & Rolls Ltd v Moore Stephens

[*Add to n.871*]   **4–263**

In *Jetivia SA v Bilta (UK) Ltd* [2015] 2 W.L.R. 1168 SC, Lord Neuberger
stated *obiter* at [30] that *Stone & Rolls* should be put to one side as "it is not
in the interests of the future clarity of the law for it to be treated as
authoritative or of assistance." *Jetivia* was concerned with the attribution to a
company of illegal conduct by a director in the context of a claim against that
director. The Court held that attribution was inappropriate in such a case, and
therefore the company's claim would not be barred. Lord Neuberger, with
whom on this point the other justices agreed, considered that *Stone & Rolls*
should only be seen as standing for two propositions; first that an illegality
defence cannot be run against a company by a third party where the directing
mind and will acted fraudulently in circumstances where the company has
innocent shareholders or directors; second, that the defence would be
available where knowledge could be attributed to a "one-man company," who
would not have innocent shareholders or directors. However, there was less
agreement about what else, if anything *Stone & Rolls* should be seen as
standing for. It seems clear that the case will have to be revisited by the
Supreme Court (see e.g. Lord Sumption at para [81]).

Such future reconsideration may take place alongside a detailed consideration
of the basis for the illegality defence, where the justices in *Jetivia* were split
between Lord Sumption, who held that a defence would arise automatically
whenever the claimant engaged in illegal activity; and Lords Hodge and
Toulson, who held that a judge would have to make an assessment of all the
circumstances of the illegal activity before deciding whether a defence arises.
Lord Sumption relied upon his judgement in *Les Laboratories Servier v
Apotex* [2015] AC 430, whereas Lords Hodge and Toulson drew on the
judgment of Lord Wilson in *Hounga v Allen* [2014] 1 WLR 2889, SC. These
two judgements provide conflicting accounts of the law relating to illegality,
and there is no doubt clarification is required.

Deliberate exaggeration

[*Add to n.875*]   **4–265**

. . . fraudulent claims.] Nevertheless Parliament responded with s. 57 of the
Criminal Justice and Courts Act 2015, which comes into force on a day to be
appointed and provides a number of sanctions, including dismissal of the
claim, if someone claiming damages for personal injury is found to have been
"fundamentally dishonest" in relation to the claim or a related claim. See
Spencer and Kinley, "The truth hurts" N.L.J. 2015, (7638), 11; chambers,
"Fundamental injustice?" 2015 S.J. 159, 18.

CHAPTER 5

PROOF AND DAMAGES

1.—REMOTENESS OF DAMAGE

(B) Proof by inference

Facts more consistent with negligence than other causes

5–10 *[Add to text after n.50]*

There is no principle in clinical negligence cases, analogous to the admissibility of bad character evidence in criminal law, by which the court can infer negligence in performing one operation from evidence of incompetence in performing others. Evidence of extraneous matters should be confined to cases within the "similar fact" principle for the traditional reason that, unless it was similar fact evidence, it was not probative of the issue to be determined.[50a]

NOTE 50a. *Laughton v Shalaby* [2015] P.I.Q.R. P6, CA (an allegation of negligence against a surgeon who performed a hip replacement operation, it having been found by the General Medical Council that his treatment of certain other patients fell below the expected standard. The CA opined that evidence of lack of probity would be relevant to the credibility of a witness, but it was the surgeon's competence that was in issue, not his credibility. The most that could be said was that any lack of probity proved could show that he would be unlikely to admit to any incompetence or that he was less likely to have followed his standard practice than he asserted. That was a slender basis on which to advance a negligence case. Moreover, on the facts, the examples of his lack of probity were not of the most serious kind. The claimant could not rely on general adverse comment in the GMC report unless she could point to other cases which could constitute similar fact evidence. On the facts, that was impossible: knee, foot and wrist operations were too far removed from hip operations to constitute such evidence. The only other hip replacement considered in the report had been criticised for insufficient discussion with the patient, which could also not be considered similar fact (see judgment at [21]-[26]).

(D) Proof and Causation

Generally

5–47 *[Add to text at the end of the paragraph]*

It was a false premise for a judge, in deciding the cause of a house fire, to conclude that if it was not arson it had on a balance of probability to be the negligence of a neighbour: the ultimate question was whether the court was satisfied that the suggested explanation was more likely than not to be true, and the approach taken did not allow for the position that the claimant had simply failed to prove the cause.

Graves v Brouwer [2015] EWCA Civ 595 (about 30 minutes before fire broke out in the roof space of the claimant's house her neighbour set fire to some card and paper in a narrow alley which separated the two properties and experts' disagreed whether that fire could have been responsible for later fire).

Applying the balance of probability test

[*Add to n.187*]   **5–48**

; also *Love v Halfords Ltd* [2014] P.I.Q.R. P20 (another bicycle accident).

2.—DAMAGES GENERALLY

General principles

[*Add to text at the end of the paragraph*]   **5–53**

There is a principle of proportionality in the calculation of damages, and it is legitimate to consider whether a benefit that is intended to be achieved by a particular item of expenditure can be achieved by cheaper means. Nevertheless, in cases where there is no alternative way to provide the claimant with proper compensation, recovery of the cost of an item of damage will not be refused on the grounds that it is disproportionate to the benefit the claimant will receive.[208a]
NOTE 208a. *A v University Hospitals of Morecambe Bay NHS Foundation Trust* [2015] EWHC 366 (QB) per Warby J at [13]-[14].

Mitigation of damage

[*Add new footnote reference 213a to "concerned" in 11 on page* [387]]   **5–54**

NOTE 213a. See e.g. *Bacciottini v Gotelee & Goldsmith* [2015] P.N.L.R. 11 (only nominal damages recovered where solicitors had negligently failed to identify a planning restriction on a conveyance of land, but the claimants had successfully made an application to remove it, and the value of the land was not affected.

3.—HEADS OF DAMAGES AND THEIR ASSESSMENT

(B) Damage to chattels, land and buildings

Generally

[*Add to n.277*]   **5–71**

The usual rule, that is that the recoverable loss for damage to a chattel is the diminution in its value on the date damage occurred, was applied in

Waterdance Ltd v Kingston Marine Services Ltd [2014] B.L.R. 141. The chattel in question was a fishing vessel which suffered damage to her engine requiring repairs estimated in the sum of £435,000. The repairs were not in fact carried out because several months after the relevant incident the claimant decommissioned the vessel thereby receiving in excess of £1m under a government scheme. The defendant's case that no damage had been suffered was rejected. It had failed to establish that no diminution in value occurred as at the date damage occurred. What if anything the claimant would recover under the scheme was uncertain at that stage. On the facts the vessel had been worth in excess of the sum eventually received under the scheme and the prima facie measure of damages was the cost of repairs.

[*Note 279*]

Coles v Hetherton reported at [2015] 1 W.L.R. 160, CA.

[*Add to n.279*]

... Civ 1704] (the basic loss was the diminution in value of the damaged vehicle as evidenced by the cost of reasonable repair; by whatever mechanism the car was repaired the claimant's loss was to be judged by the reasonableness of the overall sum paid for repair as compared with the reasonable cost of repair on the open market). See Fairhurst, "Vehicular diminution" N.L.J. 2015, 165(7637), 12.

(C) Damages for personal injuries

Actual and prospective loss

5–109 [*Note 412*]

Haxton v Philips Electronics UK Ltd reported at [2014] P.I.Q.R. P11, CA.

5–110 [*Add new footnote reference 418a to "genuine" in line 9 on page* [411]]

NOTE 418a. Where the claimant's loss includes an expense incurred, for example, by the purchase of goods or services, it is not necessary to prove that the price paid was the cheapest available. Provided the claimant acts reasonably, as where there is a real difference between what is purchased and any alternative goods or services available at a lower price, the higher-priced items will be recoverable: *Miller v Imperial College Healthcare NHS Trust* [2014] EWHC 3772 (QB) [100]-[101]).

Gratuitously provided care and assistance

5–117 [*Add to n.437*]

See also *Finnie v South Devon Healthcare NHS Foundation Trust* [2014] EWHC 4333 (QB), per Dingemans J. at [43].

(iii) *Future pecuniary loss*

Generally

5–125a An issue has arisen whether, when considering compensation for the reasonable future needs of the claimant, arising from a negligently inflicted disability, and there are a range of reasonable options, the cheapest should be selected.[469a] It has been suggested that there should be proportionality between the cost of an item and the benefit the claimant will derive from it.[469b] Proportionality in the sense that, in determining whether a claimant's reasonable needs require that a given item of expenditure should be incurred, "the court must consider whether the same or a substantially similar result could be achieved by other, less expensive, means."[469c] The basic and underlying principle however, of which proportionality is simply an element, is reasonableness.[469d] The focus is upon the claimant's *needs*, and not, for instance, the provision of pleasure, unless that is incidental to some identifiable therapeutic benefit.[469e]

A difficulty can also arise in assessing future pecuniary loss where, at the time the claimant's injury was sustained, he or she was already suffering a degree of disability which would have caused similar loss in any event. Such was the case where the claimant was being treated in hospital for an inflammatory condition which damaged her spinal cord and led to her being classified as T7 paraplegic. That injury was not tortiously inflicted but during her hospital stay, as a result of negligence in treatment, she suffered pressure sores which caused osteomyelitis, spasms and associated deep infection. On the assessment of damages it was argued on behalf of the defendant that in money terms she was no worse off than she would have been in any event as a result of her paraplegia. That submission was rejected. The trial judge was satisfied that the negligence had made her condition materially worse, particularly as regards future care needs and an award was made on that basis.[469f] **5–125b**

NOTE 469a. The issue was set out by Foskett J. in his judgment in *Robshaw v United Lincolnshire Hospitals NHS Trust* [2015] EWHC 923 (QB) at [162].

NOTE 469b. *Whiten v St. George's* [2011] EWHC 2066 (QB) per Swift J. at [5].

NOTE 469c. *Per* Warby J. in *Ellison v University Hospitals of Morecambe Bay NHS Foundation Trust* [2015] EWHC 366 (QB) at [18].

NOTE 469d. *Robshaw v United Lincolnshire Hospitals NHS Trust,* above, at [166].

NOTE 469e. ibid at [290], allowing the cost of a home-based swimming pool in a claim of brain injury; also per Swift J. in *Whiten,* above, at [262], disallowing claims for aquatic physiotherapy. See also *HS v Lancashire Teaching Hospitals NHS Trust* [2015] EWHC 1376 (QB) (claim for a hydrotherapy pool in the family home of a severely injured claimant not allowed).

NOTE 469f. *Reaney v University Hospital of Staffordshire NHS Trust* [2015] P.I.Q.R. P4, Foskett J.

The Ogden Tables

[*Add footnote reference 488a to "disability" in line13*] **5–133**

NOTE 488a. See Regan, "The Ogden conundrum" N.L.J. 2014, 164 (7630), 10 (considers *Billett v Ministry of Defence,* below, and the perceived need to depart from the Ogden formula to avoid over-compensation).

Adjustments to the multiplier

5–134   [*Add new footnote reference 489a to "cases" in the first line*]

NOTE 489a. The difficulties that can arise in applying the Ogden Tables are illustrated in *Billett v Ministry of Defence* [2014] EWHC 3060 (QB). The trial judge, Andrew Edis QC, was required to consider the effect of a relatively minor non freezing cold injury upon the claimant's future earnings capacity. He rejected the Blamire approach (for which see para. 5-136, below) on the basis that the claimant's future working pattern was not so uncertain as to justify it. However in applying the Ogden Tables on the basis that the claimant was "disabled" he drew attention to the risk of over compensation given the relatively moderate injury the claimant had suffered. He went on, at [61]:

> "my multiplier will be substantially reduced for contingencies other than mortality to reflect the minor nature of the disability. I consider that in the absence of any other evidence or guidance I should take a mid-point between the not disabled RF (reduction factor) of 0.92 and the disabled RF of 0.54, which is 0.73. There is little logic in this approach, except that it gives a figure which appears to me to reflect fully the loss sustained by the Claimant, but to do so in a way which does not obviously overstate that loss. A judicial approach to the assessment of damages involves an exercise of judgment in the individual case being considered. Sometimes statistics give an answer which appears obviously too high, given the picture which emerges in the particular case. Where that happens, the Judge has to make an apparently arbitrary adjustment to that result, or to decline to use the statistical material at all."

See further, Cottrell, "Future imperfect" 2015 J.P.I.L. (1), 42.

Loss of career prospects.

5–138   [*Add to the end of n.497*]

NOTE 497 . . . Q13, CA] In *Tate v Ryder Holdings* [2014] EWHC 4256 (QB) Kenneth Parker J refused to reduce damages on the basis that the claimant, who was injured when he was eleven, would have lived a life of irregular employment and substance abuse, observing, at [33], it is "extraordinarily difficult in any event to evaluate in any acceptable or convincing way how this particular Claimant, aged only 11 at the time that he sustained this devastating organic brain injury, would have developed" and such speculation "could be quite wrong and seriously unfair . . . "

Lost years claims

5–142   [*Add to n.510*]

The views expressed in *Iqbal* were repeated in *Totham v King's College Hospital NHS Foundation Trust* [2015] Med. L.R. 55, Elisabeth Laing J.

CAUSATION AND REMOTENESS OF DAMAGE

2.—Cause in Fact

(A) "But for" causation

[Add new paragraph to text]   **6–10a**

The counterfactual question. Application of the "but for" test inevitably involves a counterfactual question, that is, what would have happened, so far as the claimant's loss is concerned, had the defendant complied with the relevant duty of care. The complications that can arise where the duty could have been complied with in a number of different ways, some of which would have avoided that loss, some not, were examined in *Robbins v Bexley LBC*,[20a] a claim based on damage to a house from the roots of trees located in a park the defendant local authority was obliged to maintain. Nothing was done by the authority to avoid such damage after a time when it became foreseeable. The judge at first instance found that a reasonable system would have involved a cyclical reduction in the crowns of the trees by 25%, but that such work would itself have been insufficient to avoid the damage. The claimant nonetheless succeeded, on a finding that in carrying the system into effect the defendant's contractors would have gone further than strictly required and carried out more extensive reduction work, which would have been sufficient to prevent the damage. In effect, the claimant could rely upon a counterfactual finding that the defendant would actually have behaved in a more generous way than the standard of reasonable care minimally required.

Note 20a. [2014] B.L.R. 11, CA. For a discussion of the implications of the decision, see Steel, "Defining causal counterfactuals in negligence" (2014) LQR 564. The editor shares the author's concerns about the consistency of this decision with principle.

Bonnington Castings Ltd. v Wardlaw

[Add to n.33]   **6–14**

For criticism of both the "but for" and material contribution tests see Turton, "Using NESS to overcome the confusion created by the 'material contribution to harm' test for causation in negligence" (2014) 2 PN 50.

CHAPTER 6

(B) Proof of risk of harm

Compensation Act 2006, s.3

6-36 *[Add new note 62a to "liability" in the last line]*

NOTE 62a In *Zurich Insurance plc v International Energy Group Limited* [2015] UKSC 33 the Supreme Court confirmed that proportionate liability will continue to apply in *Fairchild* cases beyond the scope of the 2006 Act.

Insurance implications

6–41a *[Add new paragraph]*

In *Zurich Insurance plc v International Energy Group Limited*[68a] the Supreme Court considered whether employers' liability insurers were liable to cover the entirety of insureds loss resulting from liability in damages and costs for negligent exposure to asbestos which resulted in mesothelioma, where causation was demonstrated on a *Fairchild* basis. Where the Compensation Act 2006 does not apply the insurer is only liable for a proportionate share of the damages calculated by reference to the proportion of the negligent exposure for which the insurer was on cover. However, the insurer is liable for 100% of the insured's legal costs. Where the Act does apply the insurer is liable for 100% of the insured's damages and costs, subject to equitable rights to contribution from any other EL insurer on cover during the employee's period of employment, or from the insured where there are periods of self-insurance during the employee's period of employment. The nature and extent of these equitable rights are outside the scope of this work.
NOTE 68a. [2015] 2 W.L.R. 1471, SC.

Appraisal

6–42 *[Add to n.70]*

Fairchild was applied to a lung cancer case in *Heneghan v Manchester Dry Docks Ltd* [2014] EWHC 4190 (QB), Jay J, who observed at [79] that "*stare decisis* does not preclude the application of the extended principle to lung cancer cases, provided of course that such cases satisfy the preconditions for the application of that principle . . . in my judgment those preconditions are satisfied in lung cancer cases." See similarly the statement of Lord Hodge in *Zurich Insurance plc v International Energy Group Limited* [2015] UKSC 33 at [98] that "th[e] innovative rule of causation [in *Fairchild*] . . . is not confined to mesothelioma." It does not appear that the dicta of Baroness Hale in *Re J (Children)* [2013] 1 A.C. 680 at [41] that the "exception applies only where the claimant has contracted mesothelioma . . . a special rule, created only because of the special difficulty of proving causation in mesothelioma cases" was cited to either court, and that observation must now be regarded as incorrect.

On the facts in *Heneghan* the claimant's attempt to establish liability for the full amount of loss against each of six defendants, each of whom was responsible for a culpable exposure of less than 50%, failed. (The claimant had sought to argue that responsibility for a material increase in the risk of the claimant developing lung cancer, should be treated in law as causing the disease itself.) In the event that *Fairchild* was applied the parties agreed that the damages should be apportioned pursuant to the approach in *Barker v Corus (UK) Ltd.*, n.60, above.

Conclusion

[*Add to n.76*]   **6–48**

NOTE 76. See similar views expressed in *Zurich Insurance plc v International Energy Group Limited* [2015] UKSC 33, above (e.g. Lords Neuberger and Reed at [191]).

(D) Loss of a chance

Loss of a chance

[*Add to the end of n.86*]   **6–54**

A similar approach has been applied to a dependency claim under the Fatal Accidents Act 1976: see *Hayes v South East Coast Ambulance Service NHS Foundation Trust* [2015] EWHC 18 (QB), Chap. 16, para 16-42, below.

3.—CAUSE IN LAW

(C) Intervening act of claimant

Intervening cause

[*Add to text at the end of the paragraph*]   **6–92**

Even if a taxi driver, who drove off after realising that two passengers intended to leave the taxi without paying, was at fault, he was not liable to them in negligence where it was their own action in jumping out of the moving vehicle which was held to be the cause of their injuries.[175a]
NOTE 175a. *Beaumont v Ferrer* [2015] P.I.Q.R. P2, Chap. 4, para. 4-261, above (six passengers planned to take the taxi without paying and three successfully ran off when it came to a halt; the driver then put the vehicle in motion in part to prevent the remaining passengers doing the same but two sustained injury when they jumped out).

4.—REMOTENESS OF DAMAGE

(C) Application of the foresight test

Scope of the relevant duty

[*Note 275*]   **6–144**

Haxton v Philips Electronics UK Ltd reported at [2014] P.I.Q.R. P11, CA.

CHAPTER 7

THE STANDARD OF CARE

2.—Matters to be Taken into Account

(C) Gravity of the consequences

Sporting activities

7–28   [*Add to text after n.69*]

A claim by a ball spotter at a golf tournament, who lost the sight of an eye
after being struck by a competitor's ball, failed, on a finding that he had not
been seen by the competitor before the ball was struck and in the circumstances his presence should not have been anticipated and it was reasonable
for a warning not to be given.[69a]
Note 69a. *McMahon v Dear* [2014] CSOH 100.

(D) Cost and practicability

Social Responsibility and Heroism Act 2015[83a]

7–34a   [*Add new paragraph to* text]

The need for this Act is not immediately clear and at this stage it would appear
to complicate the task of identifying the conduct reasonably required of a
defendant in discharging a duty of care, rather than to clarify it. By s. 1 the
provisions are stated to apply when a court, "in considering a claim that a
person was negligent or in breach of statutory duty, is determining the steps
that the person was required to take to meet a standard of care." In considering
the claim a court must have regard to each of three matters set out in ss. 2 to
4: whether the alleged negligence or breach of statutory duty occurred when
the person was acting for the benefit of society or any of its members; whether
the person, in carrying out the activity in the course of which the alleged
negligence or breach of statutory duty occurred, demonstrated a predominantly responsible approach towards protecting the safety or other interests of
others; and whether the alleged negligence or breach of statutory duty
occurred when the person was acting heroically[83b] by intervening in an
emergency to assist an individual in danger. Each of these matters is a factor
which, in an appropriate case, a court would already be expected to consider
when deciding what standard of care was reasonably required of a defendant

in the circumstances and to that extent the statute is unnecessary. There is a departure from the usual forensic process in the sense that the factors *must* be taken into account, so whether any party has actually asked that they be taken into account is irrelevant: the onus is placed on the court to consider them even if no-one else has.[83c] Finally, it is not said what "having regard" to a factor means in this context: no guidance is given about the weight that must be given to the factors in coming to a decision. It is not provided that they carry greater weight than, or exclude, any other consideration which might arise in deciding a particular case and had that been intended presumably Parliament would have so provided. In the result, having had regard to the factors, the court must do what it would have done anyway and decide what the defendant's duty of care reasonably required of him.

NOTE 83a. The main provisions of the Act will come into force on a day to be appointed.

NOTE 83b. "Heroically" is not defined, presumably on the basis that heroism is self-evident, although there may be circumstances where what appears heroic to one person is regarded as recklessly undertaking of an unreasonable risk by another. See further Ch. 2, para. 2-272, and Ch. 4, 4-115, above in relation to "rescuers". And if D, in heroically trying to save A from harm, owes a duty of care to C, of which he is on the face of it in breach, why should his heroism towards A have any effect on the outcome of C's claim?

NOTE 83c. On usual principles, if by any chance, a party does not raise the matters set out in the Act it will be the duty of the court to give the opportunity for evidence to be led and submissions made in relation to them since they will have to form some part of the decision. Before a trial consideration will have to be given to the evidence required to support the proposition that the defendant was acting for the benefit of society or its members; or whether in carrying out the activity the defendant was demonstrating a predominantly responsible approach to safety or "other interests", whatever they may be. And what does "predominantly add? May there be cases where a defendant was acting responsibly to an extent, but not predominantly?

CHAPTER 8

DANGEROUS PREMISES

1. —THE PREMISES

The state of the premises

8–10 [*Add to n.36*]

In *Yates v National Trust* [2014] P.I.Q.R. P16, Ch. 11, para.11-34, below, the trial judge accepted that the defendant was not in breach of its duty as occupier, where an employee of a tree surgeon fell from a tree on the defendant's land, since the fall was caused by his pursuing the activity of tree surgery and not as a result of the state of the defendant's premises.

2.—THE OCCUPIER

Multiple occupiers

8–20 [*Add to text after n.80*]

Although the defendant owned land on which hotel premises were situated, and was a director of the company which operated the hotel, any duty as occupier was not so extensive as to make her liable for an accident caused by a defective refrigerator located in an office of the hotel.[80a]

NOTE 80a. *Shtern v Cummings* [2014] UKPC 18 (she was not involved in the day to day running of the business, which was the responsibility of the company, although her ownership of the land may have given rise to a duty of care in relation to the hotel's structure).

4. —THE DUTY OWED

(B) Extension, restriction, modification or exclusion of liability

Generally

8–43 [*Add to n.172*]

For changes to the Unfair Contract Terms Act 1977 on the coming into force of the Consumer Rights Act 2015 see Ch. 2, para. 2-214, n. 482a above.

(G) Effect of contract

Persons entering premises for the purpose of sport or entertainment

[*Add to text after n.316*]   **8–91**

A judge was entitled to conclude that where a company operating a sports ride which involved the customer being propelled into the air by plastic ropes while strapped into harness, there was a foreseeable risk of neck injury if he was not properly warned before the mechanism was operated.[316a]

NOTE 316a. *Lowdon v Jumpzone Leisure UK Ltd* [2015] EWCA Civ 586 (there was a failure to follow the company's own guidelines which required a count to three and a signal of readiness from the rider before the release).

6.—LIABILITY OF VENDORS, LESSORS, BUILDERS AND LOCAL AUTHORITIES

(B) Statutory Liability

Landlord and Tenant Act 1985

[*Add to n.433*]   **8–127**

It is a necessary implication in the covenant implied by s.8(1) that the lessor, who is not in occupation of the property, can only be liable for disrepair within the demised premises of which he is aware: see *Edwards v Kumarasamy* [2015] P.I.Q.R. P11, CA, n.443 below, *per* Lewison LJ at [19].

[*Add to n.442*]   **8–129**

In *Edwards v Kumarasamy* [2015] P.I.Q.R. P11, CA, n.454, below the landlord had a legal easement over the front hall of a block of flats, and the front hall was thereby part of a building in which he had an estate or interest for purposes of s.11(1)(A).

[*Add to n.443*]

It was observed in *Edwards v Kumarasamy*, n.442, above, that the rule as to notice in *O'Brien v Robinson* applied only where a defect arose *within* the demised premises: it was not necessary to imply a term that notice was required where a landlord's liability was being considered under s.11(1)(A) of the Act and the relevant defect existed in a paved area, not forming part of the letting.

[*Add to text after n.454*]   **8–131**

... a banister rail.[454] A short paved area leading to the front door and hall of a block of flats from the adjacent car park was part of the structure or exterior of a flat within the block.[454a]

NOTE 454a. *Edwards v Kumarasamy* [2015] P.I.Q.R. P11, CA.

The Defective Premises Act 1972

[*Add to n.460*]   **8–132**

... windows, staircases, etc]: see *Rendlesham Estates plc v Barr Ltd.* [2015] B.L.R. 37, per Edwards-Stuart J. (individual apartments in apartment blocks were dwellings if they were places where a household lived to the exclusion of members of another household; also work to the common parts of the blocks was "in connection with the provision of a dwelling" since it was in connection with the provision of each apartment).

8–136   [*Add to n.472*]

There can be a breach of s.1 if when a building is completed there are defects which, if unrepaired, will subject the structural integrity of the building to a risk of failure during its design life. "Fit for habitation" means that, on completion, the building has to be capable of occupation for a reasonable time without risk to the occupants' health or safety and without undue discomfort or inconvenience to them: *Rendlesham Estates plc v Barr Ltd.*, n.460, above.

7.—LIABILITY TO TRESPASSERS AND PERSONS OTHER THAN VISITORS

Discharges of duty and defences

8–169   [*Add to n.565*]

See Dickinson, "Open season for burglar battering: is it time to check in with the civil courts?" J.P.I. Law 2014, 2, 63 (compares the right of a homeowner to use reasonable force in self-defence as set out in the Criminal Justice and Immigration Act 2008 (c.4) s.76 and the Crime and Courts Act 2013 (c.22) s.43, with the duties of an occupier towards a trespasser under the Occupier's Liability Act 1984).

8.—LIABILITY TO PERSONS ON ADJOINING PREMISES

Liability to adjoining occupiers for progressive deterioration.

8–182   [*Add to n.595*]

. . . 13-167, below]; also *Coope v Ward* [2015] EWCA Civ 30, Chap. 2, para. 2-71, above (no breach of duty established where a wall between properties had collapsed without fault of either occupier, and it was not fair, just and reasonable to impose on one of them a liability to contribute to the unspecified cost of a replacement wall, where the wall was located on the other's land and the cause of the collapse lay on that other's side of the fence).

PERSONS PROFESSING SOME SPECIAL SKILL

1.—ACTIONS AGAINST SKILLED PERSONS GENERALLY

The "Bolam" test

[*Add to n.5*]   **9–02**

The concept of professional status is an elastic one, see Mangan, "The curiosity of professional status" (2014) 2 PN 74.

Expert evidence

[*Add new footnote reference 18a to "judge" in line 8*]   **9–05**

NOTE 18a. See *e.g. Graves v Brouwer* [2015] EWCA Civ 595, Ch. 5, para. 5-47, above (in the context of an allegation that a fire in a house was caused by the defendant's negligence in setting an earlier fire in an alleyway, an expert was asked whether, if the court took the view that arson did not cause the house fire, then on the balance of probabilities, the alleyway fire had to be the cause, even if improbable: that was a question of mixed fact and law which was not the province of the witness).

[*Add to text after n.21*]

Given the privileged position of an expert witness, a decision who is, or is not, to be treated as such has itself to be approached with care.[21a]
NOTE 21a. In *Kenedy v Cordia (Services) LLP* [2014] CSIH 76, Chap 12, para

12-200a, below, it was held that the trial judge had erred in receiving as expert evidence the opinions of a witness on issues of health and safety, where the claimant alleged an accident caused by a slip on an icy path. Opinion evidence was not justified where the facts were relatively simple and not outwith the realm of ordinary human experience.

2.—ACCOUNTANT AND AUDITORS

Scope of the contractual duty

9–24 *[Add to n.90]*

. . . 2013 4 PN 223]; also Wheeler, "*Mehjoo v Harben Barker*; specialist referrals in general accountancy practice-orthodoxy restored" (2014) 4 PN 195.

Duties to third parties in tort

9–38 *[Add to n.125]*

See *e.g. Swynson Ltd v Lowick Rose LLP* [2014] P.N.L.R. 27 (accountants who admitted negligence in preparing a due diligence report for a company considering whether to make a £10m loan did not owe a concurrent duty of care to the sole owner of the company even though it may have been foreseeable that his personal assets would be at stake).

Duty to third parties in tort

9–40 *[Add to text after n.138]*

A disclaimer appearing on the first page of a non-statutory audit report, which followed the standard wording produced by the Institute of Chartered Accountants in England & Wales in respect of statutory audits save for changing "the company's members" to "the company's director[s]", was held to prevent a duty of care arising to a third party bank in respect of the carrying out of a non-statutory audit.[138a] An accountant's does not owe a personal duty to a company director, notwithstanding that it is foreseeable that a director may suffer loss as a result of negligent accountancy advice.

NOTE 138a. *Barclays Bank plc v Grant Thornton UK LLP* [2015] EWHC 320 (Comm).

NOTE 138b. *Swynson Ltd v Lowick Rose LLP* [2014] P.N.L.R. 27, n.125 above; see also Ch. 2, para. 2-204a, above.

3.—ARCHITECTS, QUANTITY SURVEYORS, STRUCTURAL AND OTHER ENGINEERS, BUILDING CONTRACTORS

The duty of care

9–51 *[Add to text after n.176]*

Where architects provide a certificate of proper completion in in relation to building works, which a purchaser does not rely upon in acquiring the property, there is no additional cause of action available for breach of a duty of care properly to inspect the works for purposes of preparing and issuing the certificate.[176a]

Note 176a. *Hunt v Optima (Cambridge) Ltd* [2014] P.N.L.R. 29, CA, Ch. 2, para. 2-195, above, per Tomlinson LJ at [114].

[Add to text at the end of the paragraph]   **9–52**

Without an assumption of responsibility a builder's duty in tort is to protect a client from personal injury or damage to other property. The duty can be owed not simply to the first person who acquires the property but also subsequent owners or users.[177a]

Note 177a. *Robinson v PE Jones (Contractors) Ltd*, n.177, above, per Jackson LJ at [68]. See further, Chap. 2, para 2-251, and Ch. 8, para. 8-119, above. See also Carrington, "A crucial distinction" (2014) 4 PN 185.

The standard of care

[Add to n.234]   **9–72**

A construction company proposing to sink concrete piles on a site it was developing, was not negligent in failing to check museum archives before the concrete was laid to see whether there were any historic plans showing underground pipes not identified on current plans: *Northumbrian Water Ltd v Sir Robert McAlpine Ltd* [2014] EWCA Civ 685 (in fact the concrete escaped into a disused private drain, not shown on the claimant's plans, from which it made its way into the sewerage system maintained by the claimant).

4.— Auctioneers

The duty of care

[Add to text after n.253]   **9–77**

... or the potentiality of such.[253] In the case of a leading auction house a higher standard of care and skill is required than a provincial house. It is to be expected that a work of art will be assessed by specialists with ready access to art historical scholarship around the world and given a thorough examination, over a sufficient period of time to come to a firm view as to its attribution where that is possible.[253a]

Note 253a. *Thwaytes v Sotheby's Ltd* [2015] P.N.L.R. 12 (defendant not negligent in failing to identify a painting, sold at auction for £42,000, as a Caravaggio worth many millions).

5.—Bankers and Finance Companies

Giving advice or information

[Add to text after n.270]   **9–84**

So, a bank was liable to the claimant company, which operated a casino, when an employee negligently provided a positive financial reference for a customer of the casino whose balance with the bank had always been nil, even though the claimant's inquiry was made through a related company: there was no reason to restrict the duty owed to the person actually making the enquiry.[270a]

NOTE 270a. *Playboy Club London Ltd v Banca Nazionale Del Lavoro SPA* [2014] EWHC 2613 (QB) (there was contributory negligence assessed at 15% in failing to heed and act upon flaws in the shape and feel of the cheques presented by the customer to the casino which may have led to their being refused and the resulting loss, when there were no funds to meet them, avoided).

Proof of a causative link

9–95 [*Add to the end of n.294*]

... such instability]; also *Playboy Club London Ltd v Banca Nazionale Del Lavoro SPA* [2014] EWHC 2613 (QB), para. 9–84, above.

7.—DENTISTS

The duty of care

9–108 [*Add to n.341*]

A claim for economic loss resulting from alleged negligence/breach of statutory duty in removing the claimant from the list of dentists approved to carry out NHS work, failed in *Jowhari v NHS England* [2014] EWHC 4197 (QB), Sir Colin Mackay.

8.—MEDICAL PRACTITIONERS

Diagnosis, treatment and advice about risks

9–111 [*Delete heading, text and footnotes from para. 9–111 to 9–117 inclusive*]

In *Montgomery v Lanarkshire Health Board*[353] the Supreme Court identified the different approaches required when considering alleged negligence by a doctor, on the one hand in diagnosis or treatment and on the other in advising risks which the treatment may entail and the alternative strategies for treatment that are available. Diagnosis and treatment are areas of expertise susceptible to the traditional *Bolam* test[354], that is, did the medical practitioner act in a way that was accepted as proper by a responsible body of medical opinion. The test is otherwise in relation to advice about risks in treatment and alternatives. There the duty is to take reasonable care to ensure that, prior to treatment, the patient was aware of any material risks and any reasonable alternative to what was proposed.[355]

9–112 The claim in *Montgomery* arose as a result of severe injuries sustained by the claimant's son at the time of his birth. Mrs Montgomery was diabetic and small in stature. There was thereby a risk that her baby would have large shoulders and have difficulty passing through his mother's pelvis ("shoulder dystocia") without medical intervention. There was evidence that the risk if it materialised could give rise to a major obstetric emergency. In antenatal consultations Mrs Montgomery expressed concern about the size of her baby but did not seek advice about specific risks. The doctor did not volunteer such information because, in her judgment, the risk to the baby was very small and if it was mentioned the mother would elect caesarean section and that would not have be in her interests. She advised that mother would manage vaginal delivery and if there were difficulties in labour caesarean section would be given. In the event the risk of shoulder dystocia materialised in the course of the birth, the emergency which rapidly developed did not permit caesarean section, and the baby suffered injury in the course of delivery by forceps.

The appeal before the Supreme Court concerned allegations that Mrs **9–113** Montgomery ought to have been given advice about the risk of shoulder dystocia which would arise in vaginal birth, and of the alternative possibility of delivery by elective caesarean section. The claimant had failed in the lower courts on an application of *Sidaway v Board of Governors of the Bethlem Royal Hospital and the Maudsley Hospital*,[356] a House of Lords' decision which was taken in effect to provide for a uniform approach, based on the *Bolam* principle, to cases of alleged medical negligence. The Supreme Court declined to follow that decision, indicating that the time had to review, in the light of changed social attitudes and medical practice, whether the *Bolam* test was suitable in considering a doctor's alleged failure to give proper advice about the risks of a particular course of treatment.

In the leading judgment Lords Kerr and Reed emphasised that it would be **9–114** mistaken to regard *Sidaway* as rejecting any approach other than the *Bolam* test to "advice" cases. Nevertheless it appeared to give unjustified emphasis to whether a patient actually raised the issue of risks with the doctor. It achieved an unhappy compromise by applying *Bolam* as the primary test, but raising an exception that disclosure of a particular risk would be required if it was so obviously necessary to an informed choice on the part of the patient that no reasonably prudent medical man would fail to make it.[357] It was preferable to have an approach which reflected the fact that patients were adults "who are capable of understanding that medical treatment is uncertain of success and may involve risks, accepting responsibility for the taking of risks affecting their own lives, and living with the consequences of their choices."[358] There was a basic distinction between the doctor's role when providing, first, diagnosis or treatment and when, second, advising about risks and alternative treatments. So far as the first are concerned the doctor must follow the practice of ordinarily skilled members of his or her specialty. In relation to the second:

> "An adult person of sound mind is entitled to decide which, if any, of the available forms of treatment to undergo, and her consent must be obtained before treatment interfering with her bodily integrity is undertaken. The doctor is therefore under a duty to take reasonable care to ensure that the patient is aware of any material risks involved in any recommended treatment, and of any reasonable alternative or variant treatments. The test of materiality is whether, in the circumstances of the

particular case, a reasonable person in the patient's position would be likely to attach significance to the risk, or the doctor is or should reasonably be aware that the particular patient would be likely to attach significance to it."

9–115   Two exceptions were allowed:

"The doctor is however entitled to withhold from the patient information as to a risk if he reasonably considers that its disclosure would be seriously detrimental to the patient's health. The doctor is also excused from conferring with the patient in circumstances of necessity, as for example where the patient requires treatment urgently but is unconscious or otherwise unable to make a decision. It is unnecessary for the purposes of this case to consider in detail the scope of those exceptions."

On the facts Mrs Montgomery should have been informed of the risks of shoulder dystocia and the evidence suggested that, had this occurred, she would have elected delivery of her baby by caesarean section and the injuries in question would not have arisen.[359]

NOTE 353. [2015] 2 W.L.R. 768, SC. This important decision means that many cases referred to in the existing text come with a "health warning" in terms of precedent.

NOTE 354. *Bolam v Friern Hospital Management Committee* [1957] 1 WLR 582, 587. See para. 9–125, below.

NOTE 355. See below para. 9–114.

NOTE 356. [1985] A.C. 871.

NOTE 357. This aspect of *Sidaway* received some further development in *Pearce v United Bristol Healthcare NHS Trust* [1998] P.I.Q.R. P53, CA, particularly *per* Lord Woolf at P59.

NOTE 358. In *Chester v Afshar* [2005] 1 A.C. 134 Lord Walker of Gestingthorpe referred to a warning of risks being an aspect of the advice which a doctor was under a duty to give (at [92]). He also observed that during the years which had elapsed since *Sidaway,* the importance of personal autonomy had been increasingly recognised.

NOTE 359. The claimant had lost on the causation issue in the lower courts but the Supreme Court reviewed it in her favour in light of the finding that had the doctor properly discharged her duty advice would have been given that caesarean section was available as an alternative method of delivery.

Necessity of the patient's consent

9–117a   [*Add new paragraph to text*]

Border v Lewisham and Greenwich NHS Trust[368a] was a claim where no consent had been obtained to the insertion of a cannula into the left arm of a patient, who subsequently developed infection at the site and suffered permanent disability as a result. The trial judge found that in the particular circumstances the doctor had, in inserting the cannula, acted in accordance with the practice of a recognised body of medical opinion and was not negligent. On appeal it was held that a finding of breach of duty was inevitable once it was found consent had not been given, since it was implicit in the duty to warn of the risks of a treatment that consent should be obtained. The case was remitted to the judge for a finding whether, had consent been sought, the patient would have agreed.[368b]

NOTE 368a. [2015] Med. L.R. 48, CA.

NOTE 368b. It should perhaps be noted that the case had its difficulties in terms of how the issue of consent arose. At first instance the claimant did not advance the argument which subsequently found favour in the Court of Appeal. The expert evidence at trial appears to have addressed the correctness of inserting the cannula at once rather than waiting to see if it was required. It was not argued before the trial judge that if consent was not obtained, that was itself negligent, leaving only the issue of causation.

Mentally disordered patients

[*Add to n.468*]   **9–141**

... sustained injury]; also *Webley v St George's Hospital NHS Trust* (2014) 108 B.M.L.R. 190 (failing actively to guard a patient who had been sectioned and was known to present a high risk of absconding).

10.—INSURANCE AGENTS AND BROKERS

The standard of care

[*Add new paragraph to text*]   **9–182a**

The standard of care required of an insurance broker instructed to arrange business interruption insurance cover was considered in *Eurokey Recycling Ltd v Giles Insurance Brokers Ltd.*[612a] It was observed, summarising the effect of a number of authorities, that the nature and scope of a broker's obligation to assess a client's business interruption insurance needs depended on the particular circumstances, including the client's sophistication. The level of client sophistication would vary enormously and it could not be assumed that small and medium enterprises, for example, would understand the nature of the insurance. Although annual repetition of advice previously given would not be required, that assumed that the responsible personnel remained the same and that the giving of the advice could be properly demonstrated by documentation or otherwise. If a client who appeared to be well-informed about his business provided a broker with information, the broker was not expected to verify that information unless he had reason to believe that it was not accurate. While a broker was not expected himself to calculate the business interruption sum insured or to choose an indemnity period, he had to provide sufficient explanation to enable the client to do so. Such explanation should include the method of calculating the sum insured, and might well require an explanation of terms such as "estimated gross profits", "maximum indemnity period", and the relevant considerations when choosing a maximum indemnity period. The broker would need to take reasonable steps to ascertain the nature of the client's business and its insurance needs, but if providing the same type of service as in the instant case, was neither required nor expected to conduct a detailed investigation into a client's business., NOTE 612a. [2015] P.N.L.R. 5, Blair J.

CHAPTER 9

13.—SCHOOLS AND SCHOOLTEACHERS

Supervision of games or playing

9–197 *[Add to text at the end of the paragraph]*

It was negligent for a teacher supervising children at a swimming pool to be unaware for at least thirty seconds that the claimant, a ten-year-old child, was in difficulties in the water.[663a]
NOTE 663a. *Woodland v Maxwell* [2015] EWHC 273 (QB), Ch. 3, para. 3-196, above.

14.—SOLICITORS

(B) The standard of care

Importance of the retainer

9–235 *[Add to n.807]*

... the will's validity]. Per Patten LJ in *Mehjoo v Harben Barker* [2014] P.N.L.R. 24, CA at [34]: "there is no such thing as a general retainer and the terms and limits of the retainer and any consequent duty of care therefore depend upon what the professional is instructed to do."

[Add new footnote reference 809a to "understood" in line10]

NOTE 809a. It was negligent to take instructions from a client with a damages for personal injury claim by sending him several long, standardised letters to which he was to respond by ticking boxes: instructions should have been taken in a way that allowed gave clarity whether he had understood the potential extent of his claim: *Proctor v Raleys Solicitors* [2015] EWCA Civ 400 (the client was unsophisticated in the relevant field; the written advice given to him was unclear; and there were clear indications that he might not have understood that advice).

Illustrations of liability

9–249 *[Add to text after n.888]*

... to be made absolute;[888] failing timeously to agree an order for ancillary relief and obtain decree absolute for a client in matrimonial proceedings so that the order eventually obtained was rendered of no effect by the respondent's bankruptcy;[888a] [failing to prosecute effectively ...
NOTE 888a. *Stewart v Patterson Donnelly Solicitors* [2015] P.N.L.R. 7.
[Add to text after n.891]

..named;[891] failing to clarify with a client why he had chosen not to pursue a claim for a head of loss which had been identified as likely to be recoverable, where it was foreseeable that the client might not understand the information communicated by the solicitor about his entitlement to claim.[891a]
NOTE 891a. *Proctor v Raleys Solicitors* [2015] EWCA Civ 400.

Illustrations of no liability

[*Add to text after n.985*]   **9–267**

... deposit[985]; when acting in the purchase of land including a right of way over a lane which gave access, failing to make further investigations when pre contract enquiries indicated that the seller had no knowledge of any adverse claims, albeit in fact a third party had made claims in relation to the use and ownership of the lane;[985a] [in failing to advise ...
NOTE 985a. *Young v Hamilton* [2014] P.N.L.R. 30, CA (NI).

(C) Causation and Damage

"Wrong information" claims

[*Add to text after n.1054*]   **9–283**

Also, where a solicitor who had drawn up a loan agreement for a client, failed to inform him that the money he was advancing was being used for a purpose other than that he intended, there was a breach of duty, but no liability for the client's losses when the loan was not repaid because they did not fall within the scope of the duty.[1054a]
NOTE 1054a. *Gabriel v Little* [2013] EWCA Civ 1513.

Other claims arising from the negligent conduct of non-contentious business.

[*Add to n.1081*]   **9–293**

See also *Gabriel v Little* [2013] EWCA Civ 1513, n.1054, above (a loan case where the solicitor was in breach of the duty to provide information, but was not responsible for losses incurred when the loan was not repaid).

16.—VALUERS, ESTATE AGENTS AND SURVEYORS

[*Note 1136*]   **9–311**

Harrison v Technical Sign Co Ltd reported at [2014] P.N.L.R. 15.

[*Add to text after n.1136*]

A duty of care did not arise as between a tree surgeon contracted to a landowner to clear dead wood from a 150-year-old ash tree and a railway company one of whose trains was damaged when, three years later, one of the remaining limbs of the tree fell onto the adjacent railway line: any duty in tort to the claimant could not extend further than the contractual obligation to the landowner, which did not require the defendant to give advice about the general state of the tree unless, for instance, he discovered something clearly dangerous.[1136a]
NOTE 1136a. *Stagecoach South Western Trains v Hind* [2014] E.G.L.R. 59, Chap 10, para. 10-22, below.

CHAPTER 10

HIGHWAYS AND TRANSPORT

1.—HIGHWAYS

(B) Dangers in the highway

Trees and shrubs

10–22 *[Add to note 77]*

See further *Stagecoach South Western Trains Ltd v Hind* [2014] E.G.L.R. 59, per Coulson J., "I can see no basis in the authorities for the proposition that a reasonable and prudent landowner is obliged, as a matter of course and without any trigger or warning sign, to pay for an arboriculturalist to carry out periodic inspections of the trees on his or her land. In my view, that is coming far too close to making the landowner an insurer of nature." He went on to say that the authorities proceeded on the basis that a closer inspection of a tree by an expert was only required where something was revealed by an informal or preliminary inspection which gave rise to a cause for concern.

[Add to text after n. 79]

. . . not liable.[79] An educated and enthusiastic gardener with some knowledge of trees, who carried out regular informal inspections of the trees in her garden, was not in breach of duty in failing to heed or act upon the potential danger from an "included bark" union of stems of an ash tree where the tree was apparently healthy, access was difficult and the trunk covered in ivy.[79a] [Conversely . . .

NOTE 79a. *Stagecoach South Western Trains v Hind n.77 above.* One of the stems of the tree fell onto a railway line and damaged a train, having developed a crack at the included bark union. It was emphasised that the duty of the landowner was to act reasonably and prudently and that duty had been discharged by her informal inspections.

2.—CARRIERS

(C) Road Carriage

Stopping and starting

10–147 *[Add to n.441]*

. . . not to alight prematurely]; *Steel v McGill's Bus Service Ltd* 2015 Rep. L.R. 39, OH (liability for injury suffered by an 82-year-old lady where a bus moved off before reached her seat).

Child safety seats

[*Add to n.477*]   **10–159**

. . . (SI 2006/2213)] See further the Motor Vehicles (Wearing of Seat Belts by
Children in Front Seats) (Amendment) Regulations 2015/402, in force 28
March 2015.

(D) Ships

The Athens Convention

[*Add new footnote 288a to "years" in line 3*]   **10–164**

NOTE 288a. In relation to the construction of arts. 14 and 16 of the Athens
Convention of 1974 see *per* Lord Macmillan in *Stag Line v Foscolo Mango
& Co Ltd* [1932] A.C. 328, quoted at Ch. 4, n. 296, above.

(E) Aircraft

Accident

[*Note 545*]   **10–184**

Ford v Malaysian Airline Systems Berhad reported at [2014] 1 Lloyd's Rep.
301, CA.

[*Add to n. 545 after the case reference*]

It was said that if a cause that led to the claimant's physical reaction was an
event that was external to her and was one that was unusual from her
perspective, that would bring the circumstances within the description of an
accident: on the facts however the event, that is the administration of an
injection by a doctor, was not unusual and no accident arose).

Delay

[*Add new paragraph to text*]   **10–188a**

Claims for compensation for cancelled or delayed flights have become a
fruitful source of litigation and it is not proposed here to deal with the subject
in a comprehensive way, for which the reader must turn to specialist
works.[556a] Nevertheless such claims have exposed a problem in reconciling
the approach taken to the Warsaw (subsequently the Montreal) Convention by
the House of Lords in *Sidhu v British Airways*[556b] and the approach of the
European Court of Justice to claims for delay brought under EC Regulation,
and a brief summary of the difficulty is required.

Under the Montreal Convention 1999 a right to compensation for delay is   **10–188b**
given, subject to provisions limiting the amount of recovery and a two year
limitation period for claims.[556c] In 2004 the European Union, notwithstanding
that it is a party to the Montreal Convention, published EC Regulation No.
261/2004 which itself includes remedies for cancellation, prevention of

boarding and delay.[556d] The remedy for delay has been interpreted by the European Court as including a right to compensation where the delay in arrival exceeded three hours.[556e] Challenges to the Regulation on the basis that it is inconsistent with the Convention, have failed.[556f] It was also decided that the limitation period applying to claims for delay under the Regulation were a matter for national law.[556g] The two year period under the Convention did not apply. The Court of Appeal has ruled that to the extent that the approach taken in the European Court differs from the reasoning in *Sidhu*, the European decisions must, in this jurisdiction, be preferred and applied.[556h]

NOTE 556a. See articles, N.L.J. 2014, 164 (7629), 5; S. & T.I. 2014, 10(2), 36; S.J. 2014, 158(26), 9.

NOTE 556b. [1997] A.C. 430, n.555, above.

NOTE 556c. See art. 19— Delay. "The carrier is liable for damage occasioned by delay in the carriage by air of passengers, baggage or cargo . . . "

N NOTE 556d. See art. 4: "(i) . . . if a passenger is denied boarding against his will, the airline must pay compensation in a prescribed amount in accordance with article 7 and offer assistance in the form of reimbursement or re-routing in accordance with article 8, as well as meals and refreshment, transport and hotel accommodation and two free telephone calls in accordance with article 9; art. 5: (ii) . . . if a flight is cancelled, the airline must offer passengers prescribed compensation, reimbursement or re-routing and assistance in accordance with articles 7, 8 and 9; article 6: (iii) . . . if an airline reasonably expects a flight to be delayed beyond its schedules time of departure by two hours or more (depending on the distance of the flight involved), it must offer passengers assistance in accordance with art. 9 and in extreme cases reimbursement in accordance with art. 8.

NOTE 556e *Sturgeon v Condor Flugdienst G.m.b.H.* (Cases C-402/07 and C-432/07), [2012] 2 All E.R. (Comm) 983.

NOTE 556f *International Air Transport Association (IATA) v Department for Transport* (Case C-344/04) [2006] 2 C.M.L.R. 20.

NOTE 556g *Cuadrench Moré v Koninklijke Luchtvaart Maatschappij N.V.* (Case C-139/11), [2013] 2 All E.R. (Comm) 1152.

NOTE 556g. *Dawson v Thomson Airways Ltd* [2015] 1 W.L.R. 883, CA.

3.—HIGHWAY USERS AND COLLISIONS

Police

10–214   [*Add to n.655*]

. . . causative significance] ; appeal dismissed [2013] EWCA Civ 1477. See Fisher, "Boyle v Commissioner of Police of the Metropolis" J.P.I. Law 2014, 1, C5.

Contributory negligence of passengers

10–268   [*Add to n.814*]

See also *McCracken v Smith* [2015] EWCA Civ 380, Ch. 4, para. 4-261, above.

Pedal cyclists

[Add to text after "balance" in the second last line]   **10–270**

which may adversely affect balance.] A cyclist who rode her bicycle in the
centre of the road on a bend where an oncoming car had only a limited ability
to appreciate the hazard she presented, was guilty of contributory negligence,
assessed at twenty five percent.[824a]
NOTE 824a. *Sinclair v Joyner* [2015] EWHC 1800 (QB), Cox J.

Pedestrians

[Add to n.844]   **10–276**

See also *Jackson v Murray* [2015] 2 All E.R. 805, SC, Ch. 4, para. 4-40, above
(50% contributory negligence where a 13-year-old child moved into the path
of a car from behind a school bus).

CHAPTER 11

EMPLOYMENT AT COMMON LAW

1. —COMMON LAW DUTY OF EMPLOYER

(A) Introduction

Generally

11–01 [*Add to line 3 of n.1 after the case reference*]

. . . P17, CA,] also *Thompson v Renwick Group Plc* [2014] P.I.Q.R. P18 [Ch. 2, para. 2-82, above.

[*Add new footnote reference 1a to "employment" in the last line*]

NOTE 1a. For the meaning of the phrase "course of employment", see Chap 3, para 3-119 ff, above. See also e.g. *Vaughan v Ministry of Defence* [2015] EWHC 1404 (QB), William Davis J. (a marine on a training exercise, who on a day off, suffered injury when he dived into shallow water was not on duty, not acting in the course of his employment and the defendant owed him no duty of care *qua* employer).

Statutory duty to insure

11–07 [*Add to n.36*]

Richardson v Pitt-Stanley has been applied in Scotland, see *Campbell v Peter Gordon Joiners Ltd* 2015 S.L.T. 134 (the claimant, who was injured when using an unguarded circular saw in the course of his employment by a company which had no funds to meet his claim, failed in his claim against the sole director, who he alleged was in breach of a qualified duty of care not to permit the company to carry on business without there being in place an insurance policy as required by the Employers' Liability (Compulsory Insurance) Act 1969).

(B) Elements of the duty

(i) *Safe place of work*

11–23a [*Add new paragraph to text*]

The employer's personal duty to take reasonable care to ensure that an employee is reasonably safe from injury extends to travel abroad, even where the means of travel is under the control of third parties. So, where one of the defendant's senior managers was among those killed on a helicopter flight in Peru, and the company failed to make adequate or sufficient enquiry about the safety of the journey, the employer was liable, even though it was the defendant's client, which was developing the site, which was also responsible for selecting the firm from which to charter the helicopter.[113a] Also, where the deceased, a financier, took a charter flight from Cameroon to the Republic of Congo, and the 'plane crashed, his employers were in breach of duty in failing to make appropriate enquiries about safety, even though the flight was arranged by a third party, although causation was not established where those enquiries would not have revealed matters of concern.[113b]

NOTE 113a. *Dusek v Stormharbour Securities LLP* [2015] EWHC 37 (QB) (*per* Hamblen J at [174]: "The proposed flight raised obvious and foreseeable safety risks. The essential nature of the risk was unsafe operation or performance of the helicopter flight. Further, there was a real prospect of that risk eventuating given the challenging nature of the flight. Yet further, if such risk did eventuate the likely consequence was catastrophic, namely death or at least serious personal injury." Had a safety audit been carried out the conclusion would have been that the deceased was advised not to go on the flight and he would not have done so).

NOTE 113b. *Cassley v GMP Securities Europe LLP* [2015] EWHC 722 (QB), Coulson J.

Employee gaining access to or working on another's premises or plant

[Note 144]   **11–34**

Yates v National Trust reported at [2014] P.I.Q.R. P16.

Stress at work

[Add to n.362]   **11–87**

See also *Yapp v Foreign and Commonwealth Office* [2015] I.R.L.R. 112, CA (a claim based upon psychiatric injury suffered by a diplomat who was withdrawn from his role after an allegation, later found to be unsubstantiated, that he had behaved in a manner likely to damage the reputation of the United Kingdom. In the course of an extensive review of earlier cases it was pointed out that it would be generally regarded as exceptional for an apparently robust employee, with no history of psychiatric ill health, to develop a depressive illness as a result of even a very serious setback at work. There was nothing about the instant case that was sufficiently egregious to render it foreseeable that the withdrawal of the claimant from his post would cause him a psychiatric injury. It was not tantamount to dismissal, and he was told that if exonerated by the investigation, the FCO would try to find him another posting).

[Add note 364a to "reasonable" in line 7 on page [914]]

NOTE 364a. In the context of a decision to initiate disciplinary proceedings against an employee, the test is whether the decision was unreasonable in the sense that it was outside the range of reasonable decisions open to the employer: *Coventry University v Mian* [2014] E.L.R. 455, CA (it was not appropriate for the trial judge to make his own judgment of the merits of the allegation made against the claimant).

11–89   [*Delete the text of n. 372 from "Contrast" in line 10 to "decision" in line 13*]

Running unnecessary risks

11–97   [*Add to n.391*]

In both *Dusek v Stormharbour Securities LLP* [2015] EWHC 722 (QB), and *Cassley v GMP Securities Europe LLP* [2015] EWHC 37 (QB), para. 11-23a, above, the employers were held to owe a duty when procuring of chartered transportation services for their employees. Employers must ensure that the transportation providers are competent to perform the journey for which they are chartered in order that the employee is not exposed to unnecessary risk.

Employee placed with temporary employer

11–112   [*Note 441*]

Yates v National Trust reported at [2014] P.I.Q.R. P16.

LIABILITY FOR BREACH OF STATUTORY DUTY

2.—Categories of Breach of Statutory Duty

The common law duty of care

[Note 36]   **12–13**

Robinson v Chief Constable of West Yorkshire reported at [2014] P.I.Q.R. P14, CA.

[*Add to n.52*]   **12–18**

See also, *C v T BC* [2014] EWHC 2482 (QB) (no duty of care was owed by a local authority to a former employee for whom it had agreed to provide a reference in particular terms, to confine a response to police who requested information about the claimant when compiling an enhanced criminal record certificate, to the terms of the reference. There was no justification for imposing a duty of care on a supplier of information to the police which would discourage those who would in good faith provide assistance to the police on safeguarding issues [76 ff]).

3.—When an Action may be Brought

Illustrations: no intention to protect

[*Add to text after n.119*]   **12–34**

... non-resident father.118] There was no private law duty on a primary healthcare trust to protect the claimant from foreseeable economic loss as a result of a breach of its obligations under reg.10 of the National Health Service (Performers Lists) Regulations 2004 SI No. 585.[118a] There was no parliamentary intention to protect a company alleging loss as a result of an error by the registrar of companies in discharging his duty under the Companies Act 2006 to record on the register those companies against whom a winding-up order had been made.[118b] [No private law action ...

NOTE 118a. *Jowhari v NHS England* [2014] EWHC 4197 (QB), Sir Colin
Mackay (the dentist alleged that his name had been unlawfully removed from
the list of practitioners authorised to carry out NHS work; a claim in
negligence also failed).

NOTE 118b. *Sebry v Companies House* [2015] EWHC 115 (QB), Ch. 2, para.
2-95, above (although no action lay for breach of statutory duty a common law
duty of care was owed).

Further Illustrations: intention to protect

12–39   [*Replace text after the reference to Watt v Fairfield Shipbuilding and
Engineering Co Ltd as follows*]

... S.L.T. 1084, OH]. See also *McDonald v Department for Communities and
Local Government* [2014] 3 WLR 1197, SC, approving the *Cherry Tree
Machine* decision (reg. 2(a) of the Asbestos Industry Regulations 1931
extended to factories and workshops where specified processes were carried
on, it being the nature of the processes rather than the nature of the industry
which were relevant; a lorry driver who made deliveries to a power station
where lagging work required the mixing of asbestos powder with water was
potentially within the ambit of the reg.). See article, "Boost for asbestos
claims" N.L.J. 2014 (7628), 5.

Inadequacy of statutory remedy

12–55   [*Add to n.203*]

See also *Lillian Darby (Administratrix) v Richmond upon Thames LBC*, Chap
2, para 2-326, above.

4.—CIVIL LIABILITY AND HEALTH AND SAFETY REGULATIONS

The impact of section 69

12–70   [*Add to n.236*]

See generally Roy, "Without a safety net: litigating employers' liability claims
after the Enterprise Act" 2015 J.P.I.L. (1), 15.

12–73   [*Delete the last sentence of n. 240 including the reference to Kenedy v
Cordia (Services) LLP*]

Avoiding the consequences of section 69

12–75   [*Add to n.247*]

... UKHL 56]; also Limb and Cox "Section 69 of the Enterprise and
Regulatory Reform Act 2013 - plus ca change?" J.P.I. Law 2014, 1, 1.

6.—DEFENCES TO AN ACTION FOR BREACH O STATUTORY DUTY

Momentary inattention or conscious acceptance of risk

12–89   [*Add to n.293*]

... para 6-87 et seq, above.] See also *Fulton v Vion Food Group Ltd* [2015]
NICA 10 (where a safety glove worn by a butcher was cut by a knife he

himself was using and shortly after he sustained an injury as a result of a further cut through the hole, the employer was found in breach of the Personal Protective Equipment at Work Regulations (Northern Ireland) 1993, but the sole cause of the accident was held to be the employee's own failure to alert his employer to the defect, notwithstanding a clear instruction for him to do so.

7.—Examples of Statutory Duty

(C) The Management of Health and Safety at Work Regulations 1999

Risk assessment

[*Add to n.379*]   12–120

It was pointed out in *Kenedy v Cordia (Services) LLP* [2014] CSIH 76 that since s.3(1) of the Management of Health and Safety at Work Regulations 1999 did not impose a duty to take precautions, a breach of the duty it did impose could not be said to be causative of an injury alleged to arise as a result of precautions not being taken.

(D) The Workplace (Health, Safety and Welfare Regulations) 1992

The workplace

[*Add new footnote reference 445a to "is" in the last line*]   12–139

Note 445a. See *e.g. Coia v Portavardie Estates Ltd* 2015 Rep. L.R. 22, IH (where the defendant, an hotelier and lodge operator, provided its employee, the claimant, with a lodge, on the basis he should vacate it if a customer required it, the premises were not the claimant's workplace when, in the course of removing his personal possessions, he was injured by a loose pole in a cupboard).

Floors and traffic routes

[*Add to the end of n.504*]   12–153

... the regulations]; appeal dismissed [2014] 3 WLR 1197, SC).

(E) The Work at Height Regulations 2005

Who is liable

[*Note 613*]   12–177

Yates v National Trust reported at [2014] P.I.Q.R. P16.

(G) The Provision and Use of Work Equipment Regulations 1998

Who is covered

[*Add new paragraph to text*]   12–200a

The scope of the Provision and Use of Work Equipment Regulations 1992, predecessor to the Work Equipment Regulations of 1998, was considered in a claim against her employer by a home carer who, in the course of her employment, lost her footing on an icy path. It was said that the obligations under the regulations were focused on work-related risks, not risks to which any member of the public may be exposed. Accordingly there was no duty on her employer to provide the claimant with personal protective equipment aimed at reducing the risk of her slipping on snow or ice.[684a]

Note 684a. *Kenedy v Cordia (Services) LLP* [2014] CSIH 76 (the claimant alleged a breach of reg.4 of the 1992 Regulations).

Work equipment

12–206   [*Add to n.693*]

... 39, OH]; also *Coia v Portavardie Estates Ltd* 2015 Rep. L.R.22, IH, para 12–139, above (a loose pole in a cupboard, in a lodge provided to the claimant by his employer, which came away while he was moving his possessions, was not work equipment).

(K) The Manual Handling Operations Regulations 1992

The duty

12–268   [*Add to text after n.910*]

... bags of cement]; in a bus yard, the use of a mechanical gritter would have avoided the risk of injury inherent in spreading grit by hand, but the defendant failed to advance any defence that it was not reasonably practicable to avoid that particular manual handling operation.[910a] [An employer ...

Note 910a. *King v RCO Support Services Ltd.*, n.891, above.

12–269   [*Delete text to n.914*]

[*Add to text after n.913*]

... manual handling operation]; where a learning support assistant injured her back in pushing a pupil in her wheelchair, but it was not reasonably practicable to avoid the use of manual wheelchairs and suitable risk assessments had been performed.[914]

Note 914. *Sloan v Rastrick High School Governors* [2015] P.I.Q.R. P1, CA.

12–276   [*Add to text after n.925*]

In contrast, where no satisfactory risk assessment had been performed, but an accident happened which was unconnected with any risk which the assessment would have identified or addressed, there was no liability. There was no causal connection between the breach of duty and the damage which in fact occurred.[925a]

Note 925a. *West Sussex CC v Fuller* [2015] EWCA Civ 189 (the claimant employee tripped on a staircase while she was delivering post around the office, no risk assessment had been carried out but she was not overloaded and the trip was the result of a simple misjudgement in placing her feet).

DANGEROUS THINGS: RYLANDS V FLETCHER

1.—PRINCIPLES OF LIABILITY

(A) Introduction

The rule in Rylands v Fletcher

[*Add to n.13*]   **13–06**

See further *Northumbrian Water Ltd v Sir Robert McAlpine Ltd* [2014] EWCA
Civ 685, Chap. 9, para. 9-72, above (no liability in nuisance, *Rylands* not
being relied upon, for an escape of concrete into the claimant's sewer, in the
course of building work carried out by the defendant).

3.—WATER

Water undertakers' liability for escapes from pipes

[*Add to n.302*]   **13–85**

In *Nicholson v Thames Water Utilities Ltd* [2014] EWHC 4249 (QB), a claim
for damage caused by an escape of sewage into domestic premises from the
main sewer, the water undertaker was not liable under s.209(1) since, per
Knowles J at [39]: "The language of subsection (1) makes plain the section
concerns an entity in its capacity as a water undertaker not as a sewerage
undertaker.

Sewers and drains

[*Add to n.315*]   **13–90**

It should be noted that there is separate provision in the Water Industry Act
1991 for the duties and liabilities of water undertakers (for whom see paras

13–84 ff above) and sewage undertakers. Thus in *Nicholson v Thames Water Utilities Ltd* [2014] EWHC 4249 (QB), para. 13–85, above, it was pointed out that even if the defendant was both a water and sewage undertaker, liability for an escape of sewage could not attach because the pipe from which escape occurred was vested in the defendant qua water undertaker, not otherwise.

CHAPTER 15

PRODUCT LIABILITY

2.—GENERAL PRINCIPLES OF LIABILITY

(A) Under the Consumer Protection Act 1987: Part 1 "Product Liability"

Expectation of Consumers

[Add to text after n.68]   **15–20**

The claimant need not specify with precision or accuracy the exact way that the product is defective, but instead that it had fallen below the level of safety which could be generally expected of the product.[68a]
NOTE 68a. *Hufford v Samsung Electronics (UK) Ltd* [2014] EWHC 2956 (TCC).

Defect and Causation

[Add to n.102 after the case reference in line 1]   **15–30**
. . . P13, CA]; also *Love v Halfords Ltd* [2014] P.I.Q.R. P20. [See further . . .

[Add to text at end of paragraph]

The claimant cannot recover for damage to property in circumstances where expert evidence suggests that fire which caused the damage originates outside of the product.[102a]
NOTE 102a *Hufford v Samsung Electronics (UK) Ltd* [2014] EWHC 2956 (TCC), para 15-20, above.

3.—LIABILITY IN CONTRACT

Strict Liability

[Add new n.174a to "included" in the last line]   **15–53**

NOTE 174a. On the coming into force of Chapter 2 of Part 1 of the Consumer Rights Act 2015 terms will be implied into a contract by which a trader is to supply goods to a consumer. A consumer is defined in s.2(3) as "an individual acting for purposes that are wholly or mainly outside that individual's trade, business, craft or profession"; and a trader is defined in s.2(2) as "a person acting for purposes relating to that person's trade, business, craft or profession, whether acting personally or through another person acting in the trader's name or on the trader's behalf." In such contracts the Sale of Goods Act 1979 will no longer be the source of the traders' obligation to supply goods of satisfactory quality and which are fit for purpose. These will be implied into consumer contracts by ss. 9 and 10 of the Consumer Rights Act. The Sale of Goods Act 1979 will continue to be the source of implied obligations in contracts between traders.

CHAPTER 16

DEATH AND CAUSES OF ACTION

1.—THE COMMON LAW

The rules at common law

[Note 11]   16–02

Haxton v Philips Electronics UK Ltd reported at [2014] P.I.Q.R. P11, CA.

2.—THE ACCRUAL OF A CAUSE OF ACTION

(A) The Fatal Accidents Act 1976

No presumption of pecuniary loss

[Add to n.135]   16–43

See *e.g.* n.138a, below.

Where marriage has been annulled or dissolved or parties are judicially separated

[Add to text at the end of the paragraph]   16–42

. . . can be taken into account.] Where it was accepted that the claimant, the former wife of the deceased, had been on the point of reconciliation with him, dependency was assessed on the basis of an 80% chance that a reconciliation would have been permanent.[138a]
NOTE 138a. *Hayes v South East Coast Ambulance Service NHS Foundation Trust* [2015] EWHC 18 (QB).

Other considerations in ascertaining pecuniary loss

[Note 144]   16–43

Haxton v Philips Electronics UK Ltd reported at [2014] P.I.Q.R. P11, CA.

INSURANCE AND OTHER COMPENSATION SCHEMES

1.—Compulsory Insurance

(A) Motor Insurance

Motor Insurance

17–03 [*Add to n.*6]

. . . April 3, 2000.] In *Vnuk v Zavarovalnica Triglav dd* (C-162/13) the ECJ decided that the compulsory third party motor insurance requirement under art.3 of Directive 72/166 was applicable to the use of a tractor on a private farm yard. See further Bevan, "Ignore at your peril" N.L.J. 2014, (7628), 7.

Exceptions in English and Welsh cases

17–15 [*Add to n.*47]

. . . sell the drugs illegally.] However in *Delaney v Secretary of State for Transport* [2015] EWCA Civ 172 it was held in the Court of Appeal that cl.6.1(e)(iii) of the Uninsured Drivers' Agreement was itself in breach of the UK's obligations under European Directives, namely Directive 72/166, Directive 84/5 and Directive 90/232. The decision of the trial judge that the breach was sufficiently serious to entitle the claimant to *Francovich* damages (cf Ch. 4, para. 4-244, above) was upheld.

3.—Criminal Injuries Compensation

The new scheme

17–32 [*Add to n.*101]

See *RS v Criminal Injuries Compensation Authority* [2014] 1 W.L.R. 1313, CA, in which it was said that caution should be exercised in drawing assistance from common law cases when considering the words "immediate aftermath", see Ch.2, para.2-152 above.

Crime of violence

[Note 103]   **17–33**

CICA v First-Tier Tribunal (Social Entitlement Chamber) reported at [2014] P.I.Q.R. P10, CA.

[Add new footnote reference 103a to "foetus" in sub paragraph 4(1)(e)]

NOTE 103a. Under an earlier Scheme a mother's excessive consumption of alcohol, causing her child to be born with permanent damage from foetal alcohol spectrum disorder, did not entitle the child to compensation, since the child had no separate legal personality when the damage occurred: *CP v Criminal Injuries Compensation Authority* [2015] 2 W.L.R. 463, CA.

[Note 105]   **17–34**

CICA v First-Tier Tribunal (Social Entitlement Chamber) reported at [2014] P.I.Q.R. P10, CA.

Procedure for making applications

[Add to n.126]   **17–41**

See *Colefax v First Tier Tribunal (Social Entitlement Chamber)*[2014] P.I.Q.R. P21, CA (the CICA was entitled not to waive the two year time limit where, although a link between an applicant's epilepsy and an assault upon him was only diagnosed after two years, he had suffered other serious injuries in the incident and an application could and should have been made earlier. It was said that while paras. 53, 56 and 57 of the scheme made some provision for satisfying claims in respect of late manifested or diagnosed injuries by reappraisal, they did not assist a victim where a serious injury manifested itself, or was first diagnosed as caused by an incident, more than two years after, where an application for compensation had not already been brought on time. Compensation for such an applicant had to rest on satisfying the conditions imposed by paras.18 (a) and (b) and even then, the waiver of the time limit was a matter of discretion for the authority).